Art for the
New Collector
IV

Art for the New Collector IV

July 12 through September 10, 2005

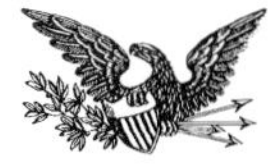

Spanierman Gallery, LLC

www.spanierman.com

45 East 58th Street   New York, NY 10022
Telephone (212) 832-0208   Fax (212) 832-8114
ginagreer@spanierman.com

Published in the United States of America in 2005 by
Spanierman Gallery, LLC, 45 East 58th Street, New York, NY 10022.

ISBN 0-945936-70-2

Design: Marcus Ratliff
Photography: Roz Akin
Composition: Amy Pyle
Printing: Capital Offset

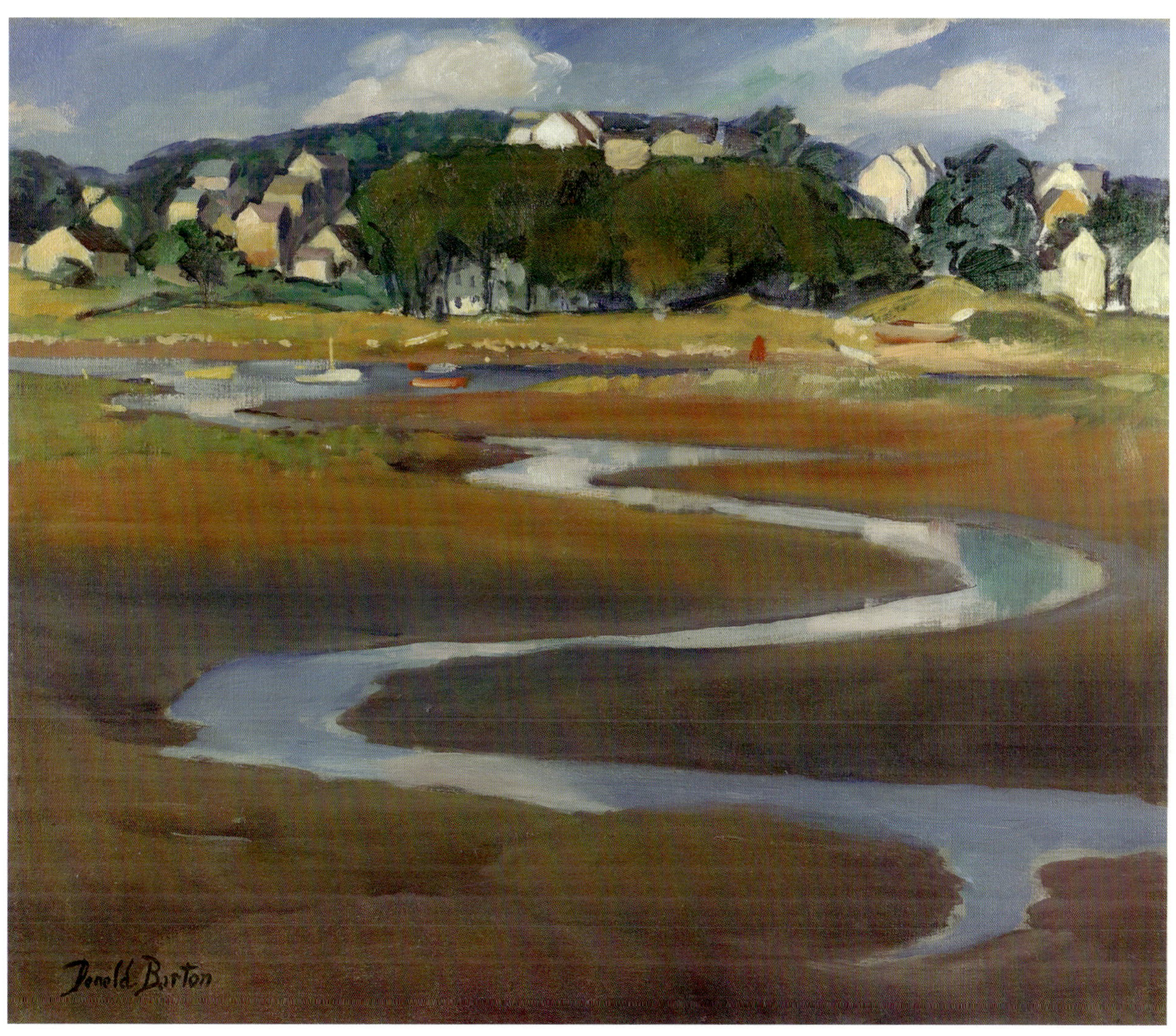

1.

Donald Blagge Barton
(1903–1990)
*Tidal River, Cape Ann,
Massachusetts*, 1927
Oil on canvas
20 × 24 inches
Signed lower left:
Donald Barton

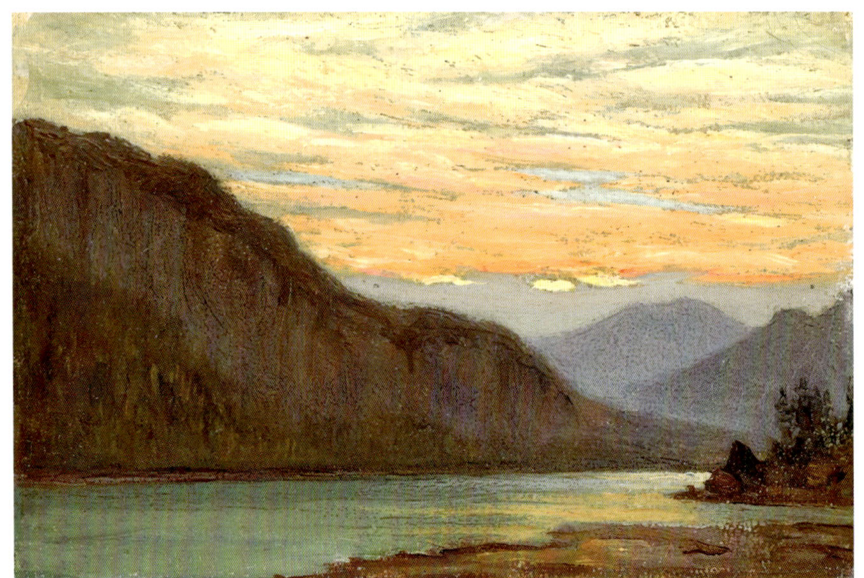

2.
American School
(19th century)
Landscape Study:
Clark Fork River near
Montana, ca. 1880s
Oil on board
3 × 4½ inches

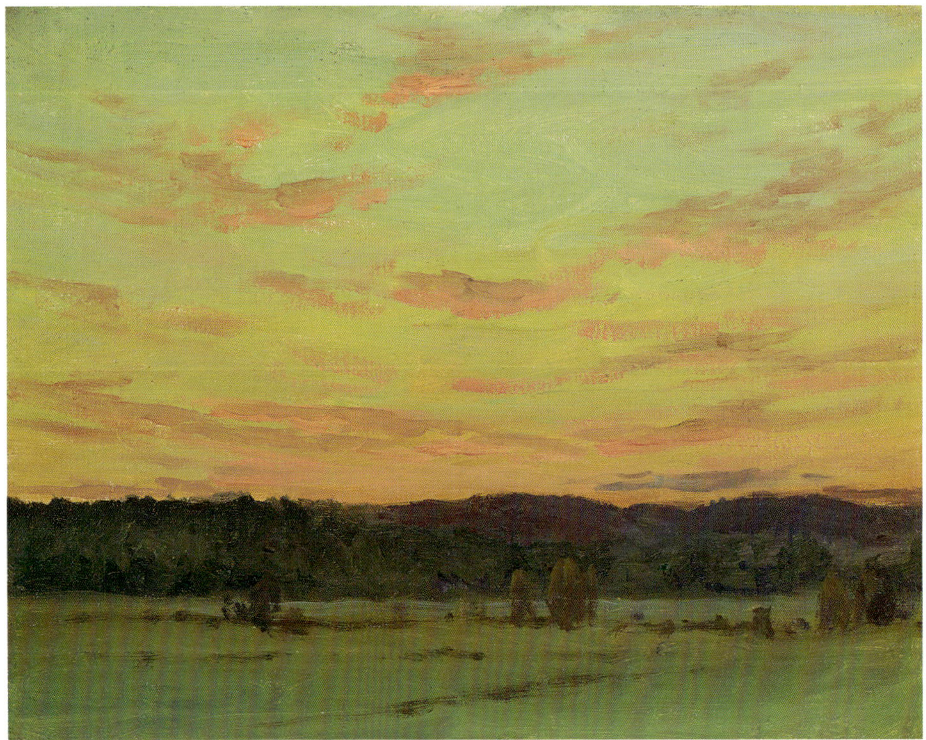

3.
Charles Warren Eaton
(1857–1937)
Sky Study, ca. 1910–20
Oil on canvas mounted
on board
10½ × 13¾ inches

4.
Henry Farrer (1843–1903)
Pond at Dusk (probably
New York), 1896
Watercolor on paper
8¾ × 12 inches
Signed and dated lower
left: *H. Farrer. 1896.*

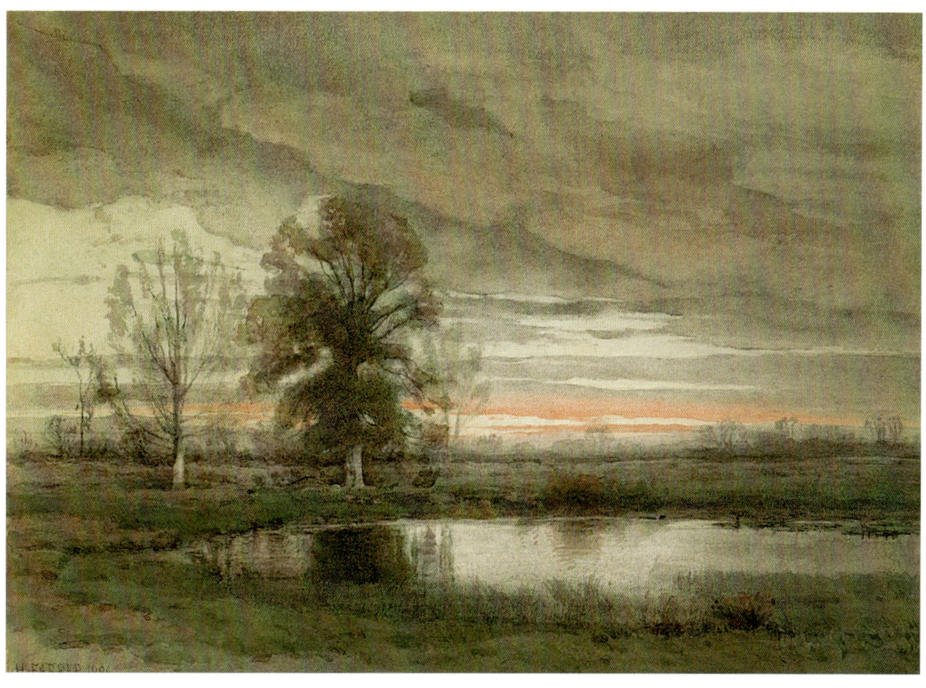

5.
Theodore Wores
(1859–1939)
Sky, Earth, and Water,
ca. early 1930s
Oil on canvas
8½ × 12½ inches
Signed lower right:
Theodore Wores

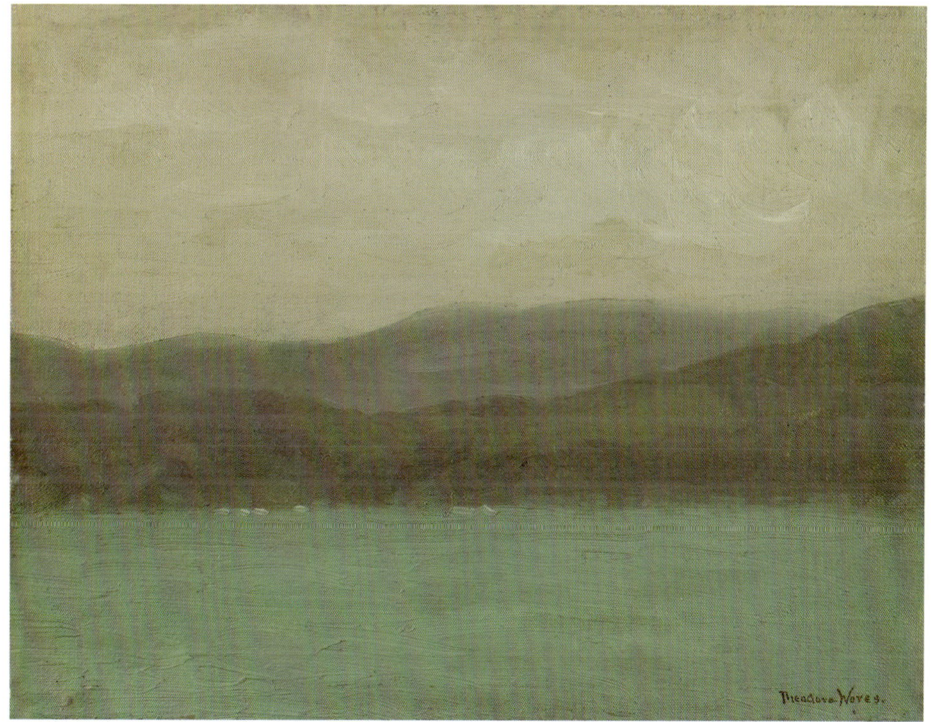

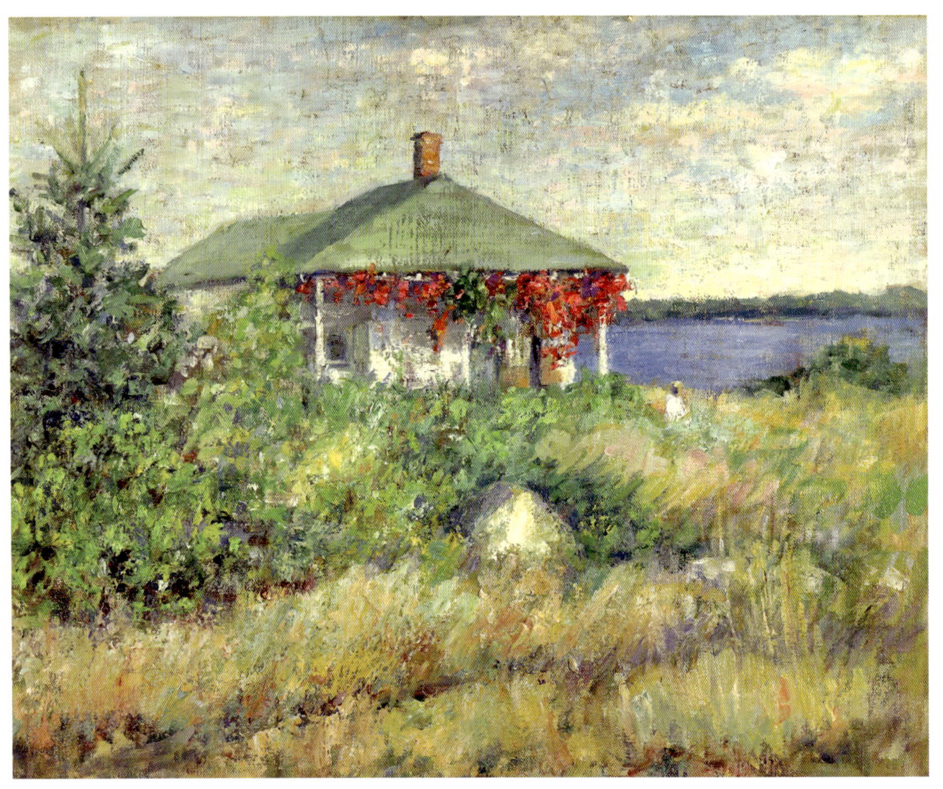

6.
Isabelle H. Ferry
(1865–1937)
Cottage by the Sea
(probably Boothbay
Harbor, Maine), ca. 1900s
Oil on canvas
16 × 20 inches
Estate stamp on verso

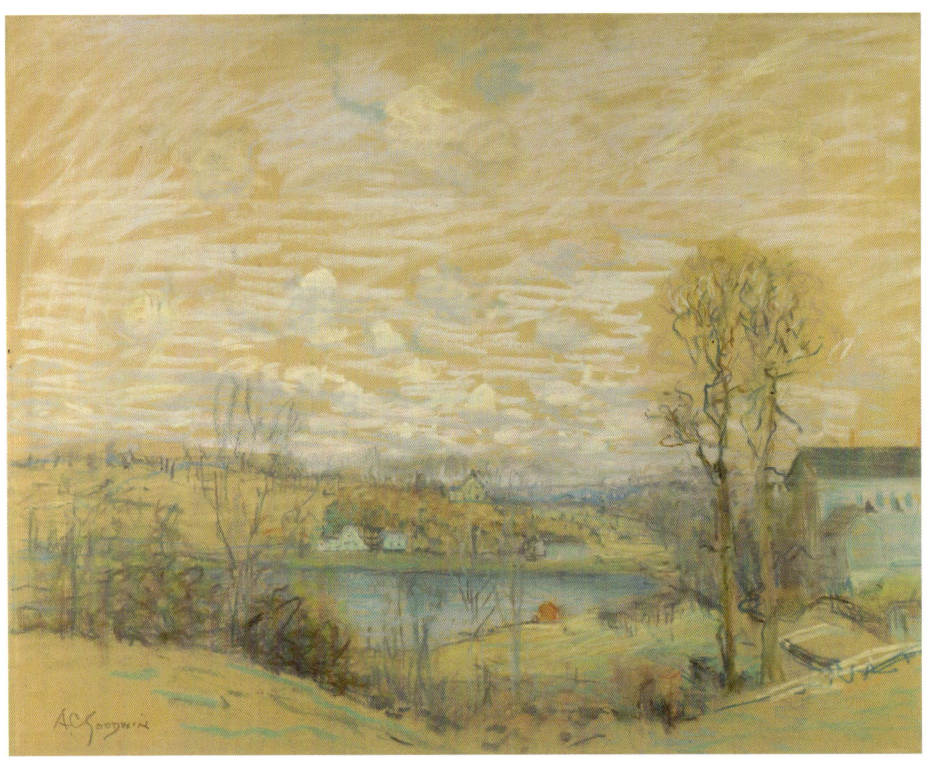

7.
Arthur Clifton Goodwin
(1864–1929)
View of Old Chatham
(New York), ca. 1920–29
Pastel on board
18⅛ × 23⅜ inches
Signed lower left:
A C Goodwin

8.
James Arthur Merriam
(1880–1951)
*Coastal Landscape,
California,* ca. 1920–30
Oil on canvas
12 × 14 inches
Signed lower right: *James
Merriam*

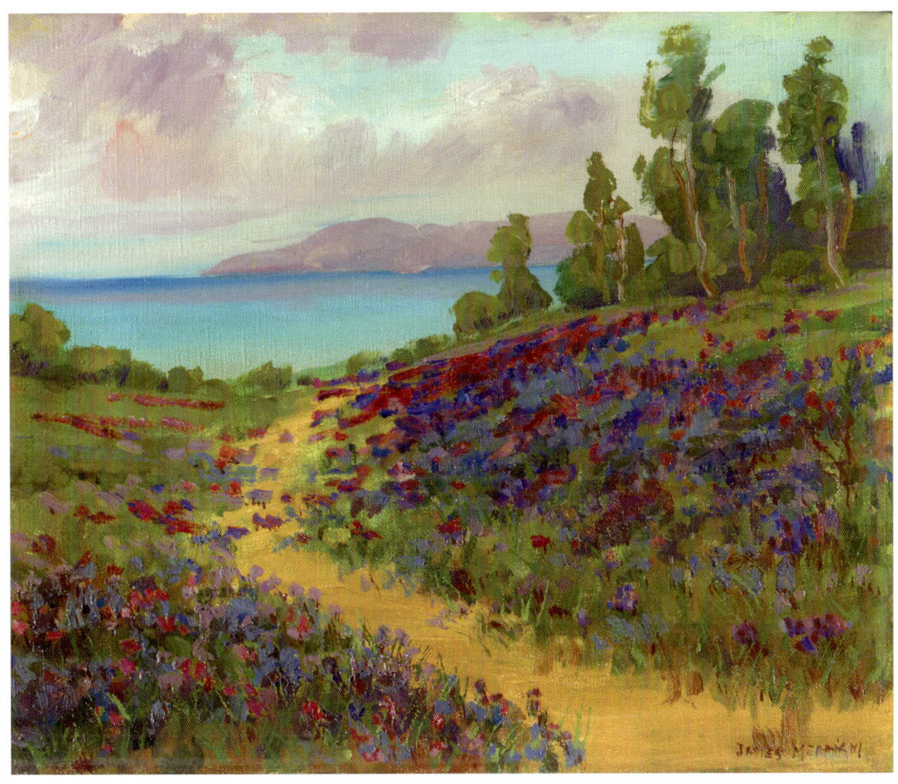

9.
**Marie Henrietta Osthaus
Griffith** (1855–1927)
Peonies in Bloom, ca. 1910
Oil on canvas
18 × 24 inches
Signed lower left: *Marie
Osthaus Griffith.*

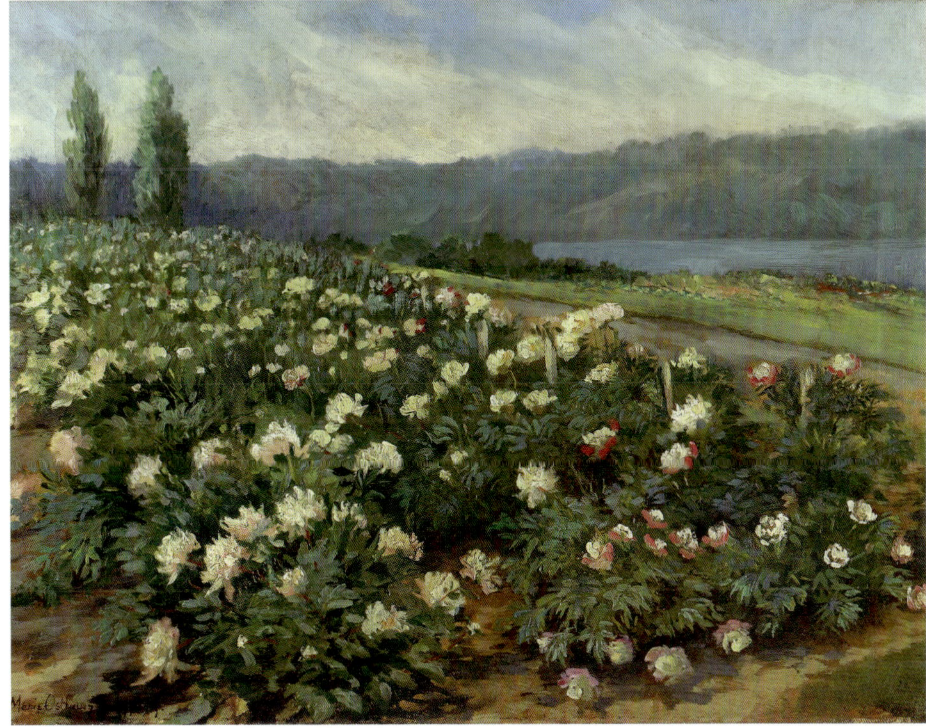

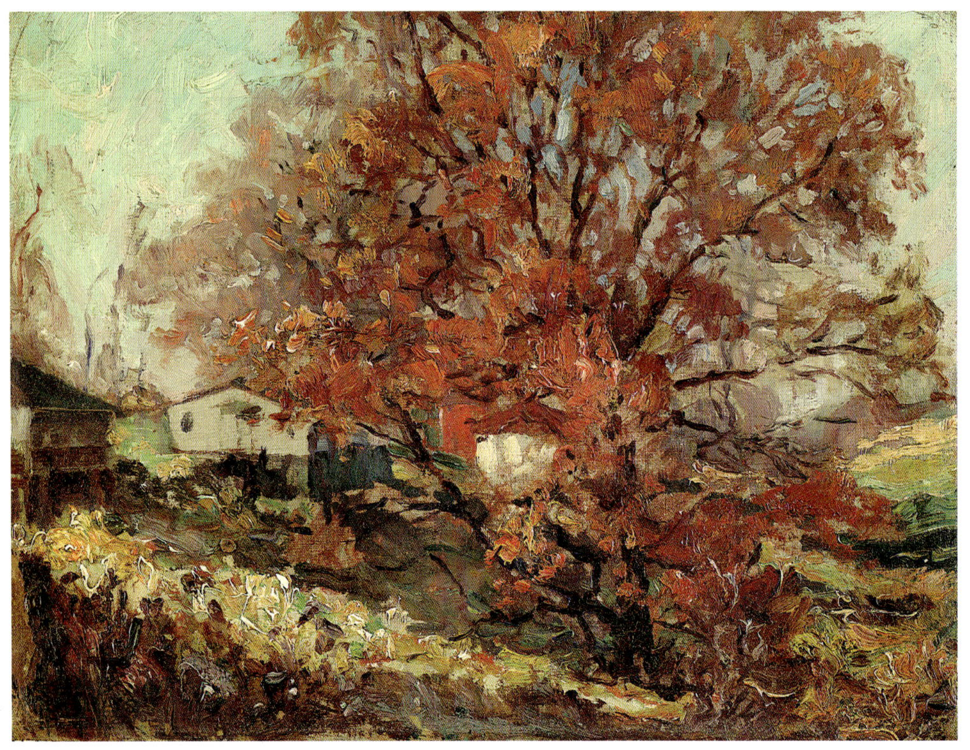

10.
Glenn C. Sheffer
(1881–1948)
Summertime Cottages, 1927
Oil on canvasboard
12 × 16 inches
Signed and dated lower
left: *Glen Sheffer / 27*;
Signed, dated, and
inscribed on verso: *Glen
Sheffer / "Summertime
Cottages"*

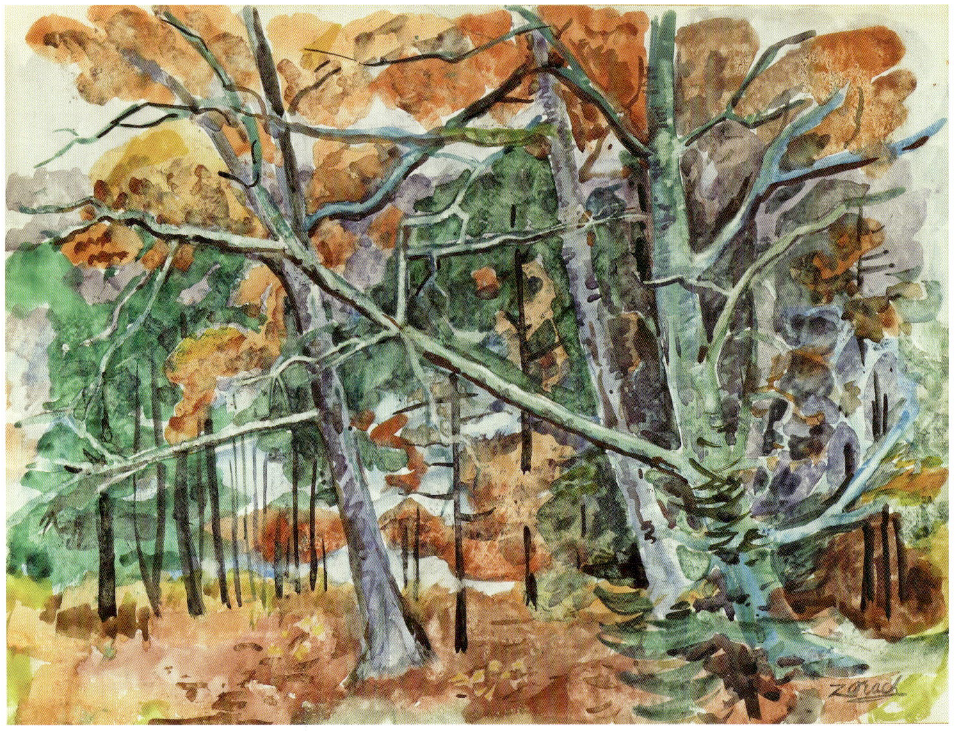

11.
William Zorach
(1887–1966)
Autumn Oaks, 1953
Watercolor on paper
17 × 12 inches
Signed lower right: *Zorach*

12.
Walter Clark (1848–1917)
*Hunter's View of the
Homestead* (probably
Connecticut), ca. 1900–10
Oil on canvas
16¼ × 20¼ inches
Signed lower right:
Walter Clark

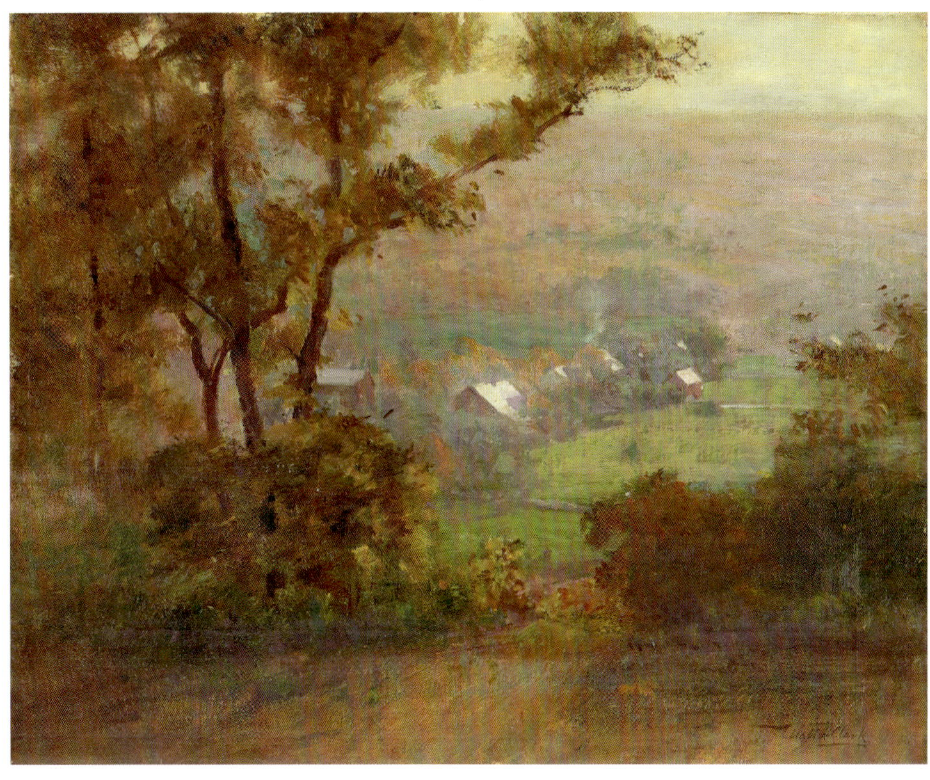

13.
George Herbert Baker
(1878–1943)
Vivid Autumn (probably
Indiana), ca. 1890s
Oil on panel
20 × 16 inches
Signed lower left:
G. H. Baker

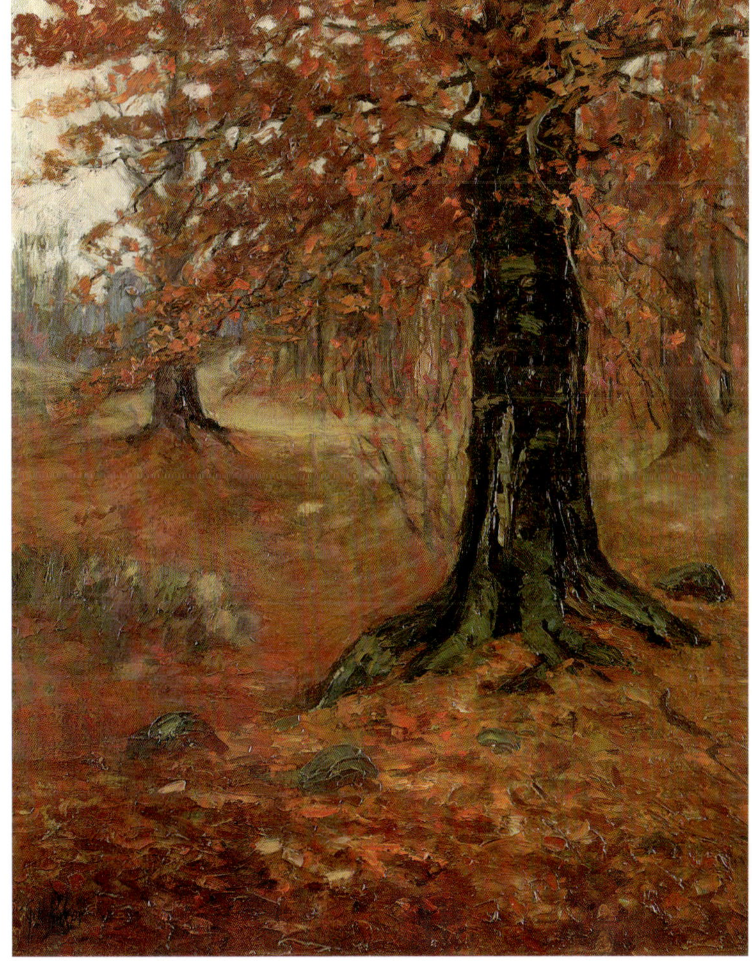

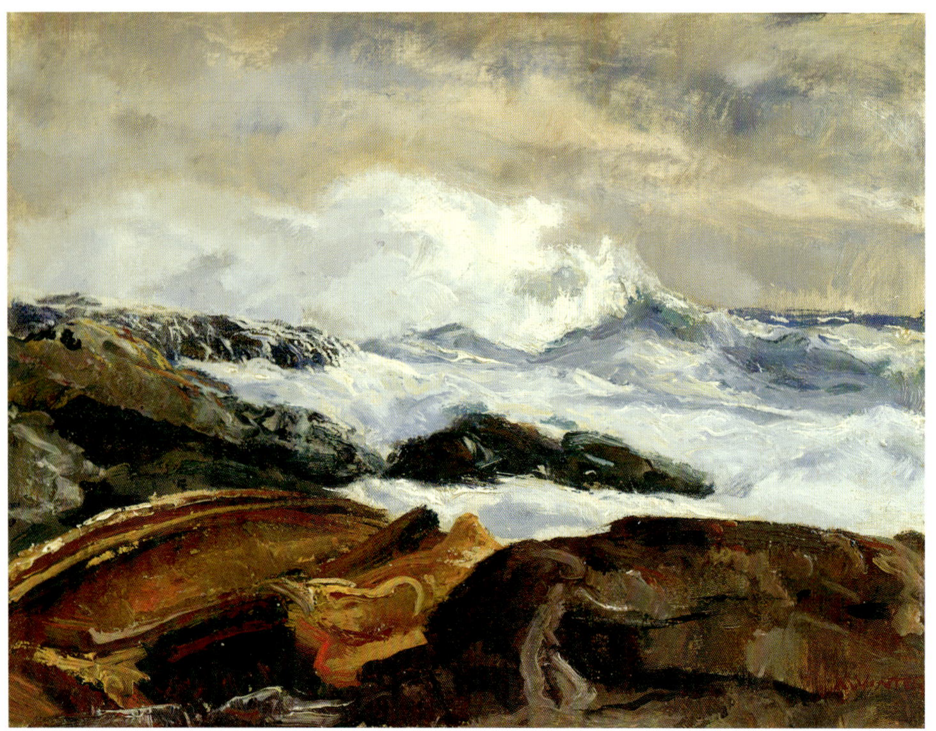

14.
Andrew Winter (1892–1958)
Monhegan Surf (Maine),
ca. 1940s
Oil on board
12 × 16 inches
Signed lower right:
A Winter

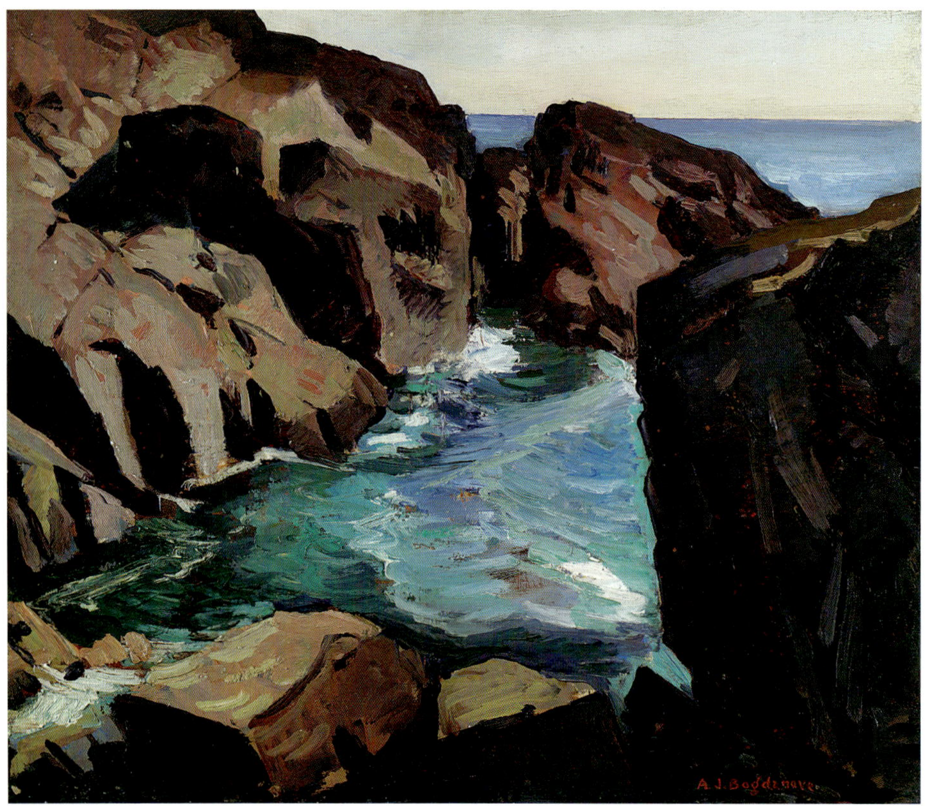

15.
Abraham J. Bogdanove
(1886–1946)
Gull Pond (Monhegan
Island, Maine), 1945
Oil on canvas mounted
on board
20 × 24 inches
Signed lower right:
A. J. Bogdanove
Dated and inscribed on
verso: *45 / Gull Pond*

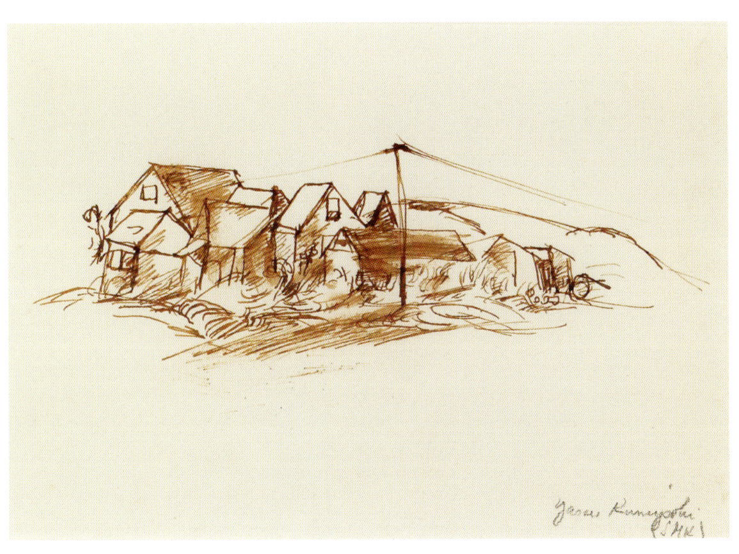

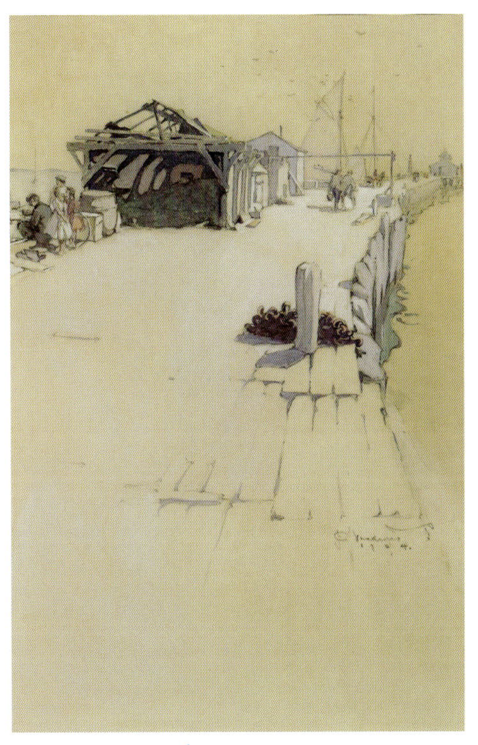

16.
Yasuo Kuniyoshi (1893–1953)
Maine Shacks, ca. 1920s
Ink on paper, 6½ × 9½ inches
Signed lower right: *Yasuo Kuniyoshi SMK*
[Sara M. Kuniyoshi]

17.
John C. Vondrous (1884–1935)
Provincetown Pier with Artist Sketching
(Massachusetts), 1904
Watercolor on paper, 12 × 9½ inches
Signed with the artist's monogrammed
signature and dated lower right: *J. C.
Vondrous / 1904.*

18.
Abraham J. Bogdanove
(1886–1946)
The Flake Yard (Monhegan
Island, Maine), 1943
Oil on masonite
9⅛ × 12 inches
Signed and dated lower
right: *A. J. Bogdanove / '43*

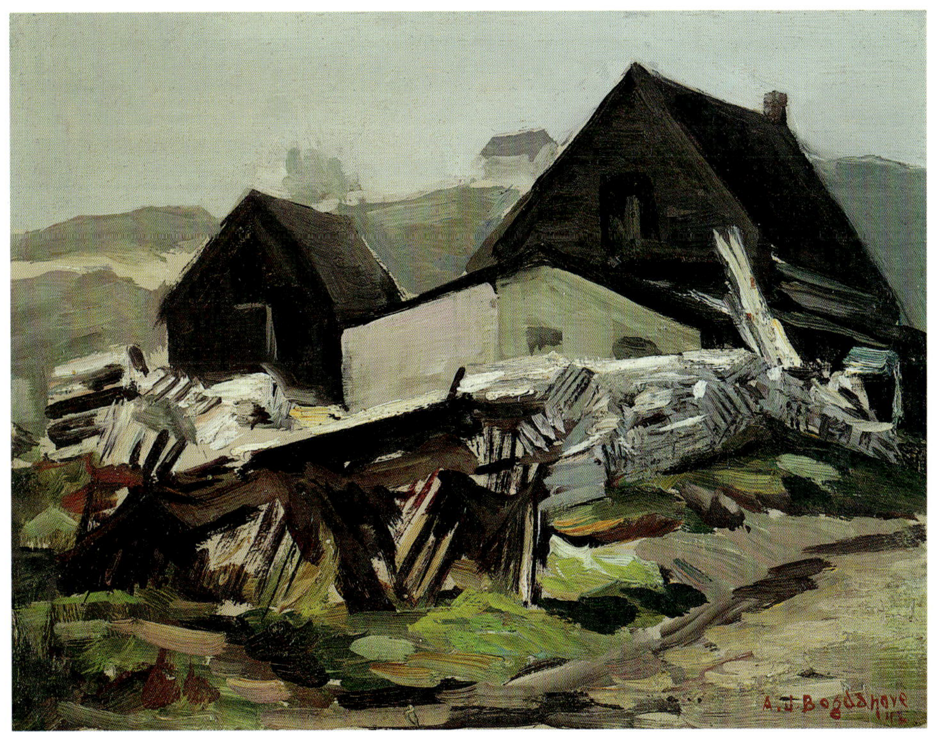

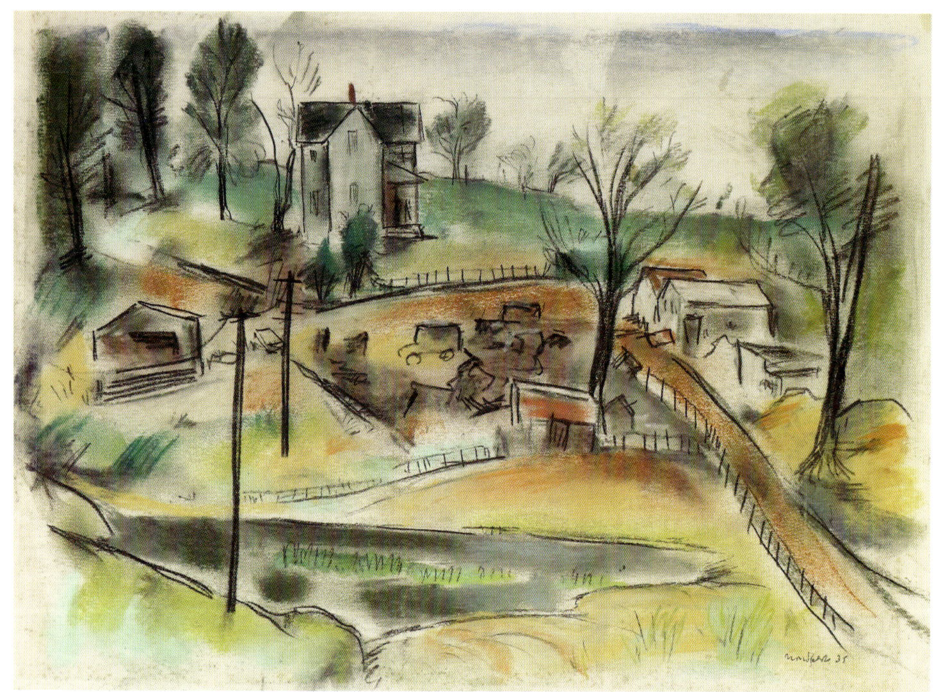

19.
Bror Julius Olsson Nordfeldt (1878–1955)
Expansive Farm, 1935
Pastel on paper
12 × 16 inches
Signed lower right:
Nordfeldt 35

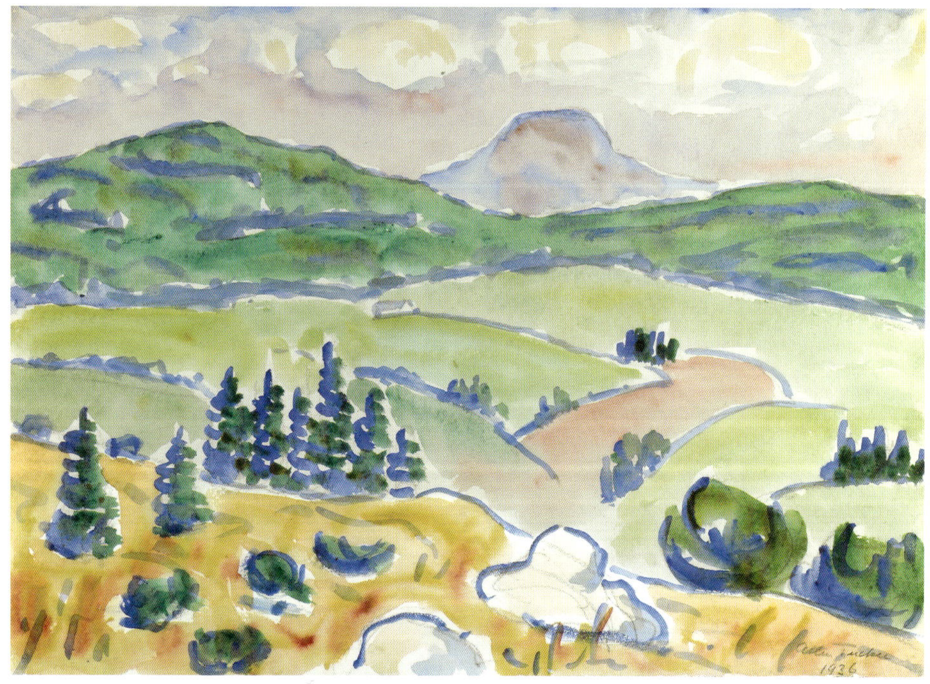

20.
Allen Tucker (1866–1939)
Hills at Castine
(Maine), 1936
Watercolor on paper
14 × 20 inches
Signed and dated lower
right: *Allen Tucker / 1936*

21.
**Harold Christopher
Davies** (1891–1976)
View from a Hilltop,
ca. 1930
Watercolor on paper
12⅞ × 15⅞ inches
Stamped with the artist's
monogrammed initials
lower left and lower right:
HCD

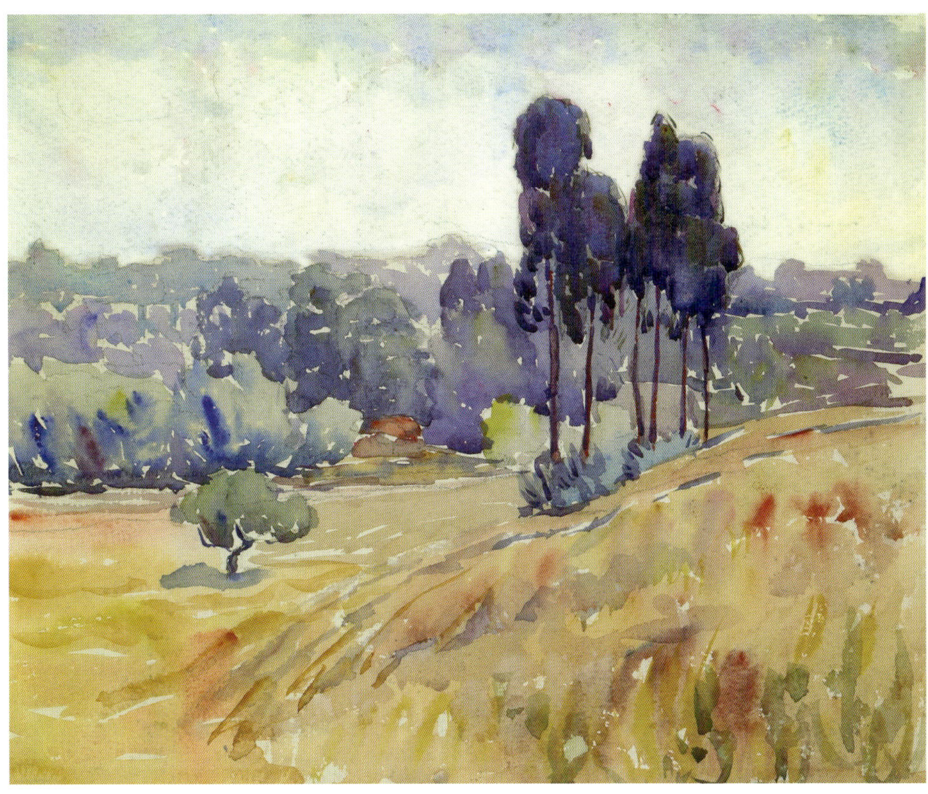

22.
Allen Tucker (1866–1939)
In the Desert (New
Mexico), ca. 1925
Watercolor on paper
13¾ × 9¼ inches
Signed lower center:
Allen Tucker

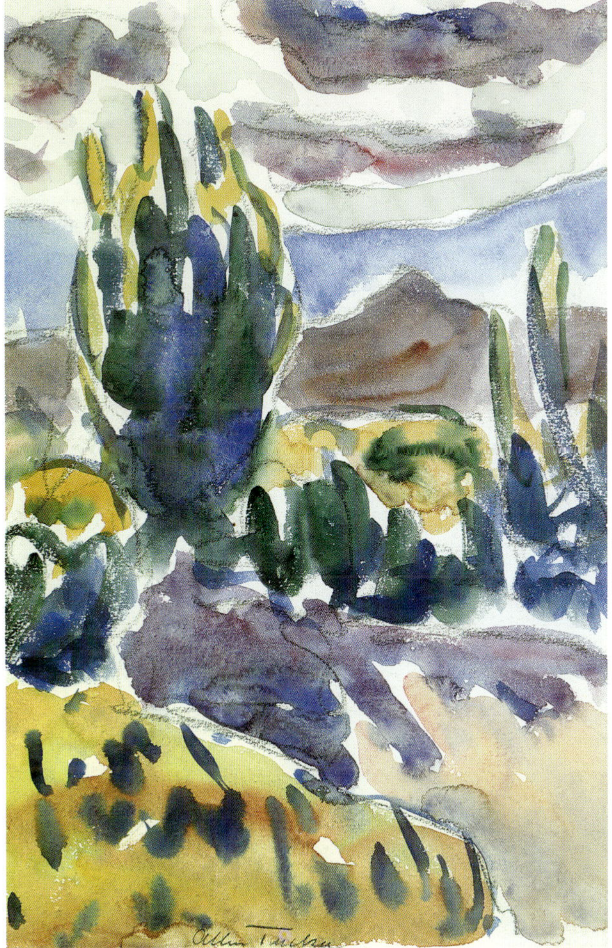

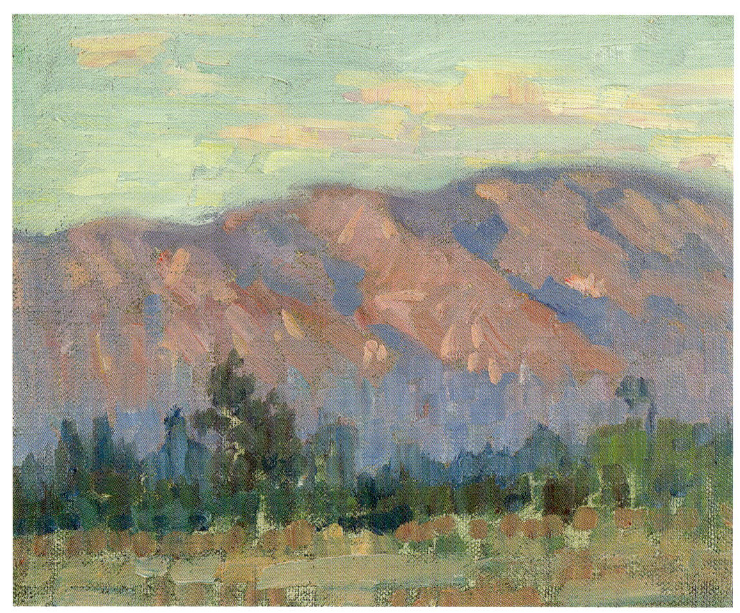

23.
Alson Skinner Clark
(1876–1949)
*San Gabriel Mountains,
California*, 1924
Oil on board
7½ × 9½ inches
Dated and inscribed on
estate label on verso:
*Mountains, California. /
Date 1924, Size 7 x 9*; Dated
and inscribed on verso:
Mountains 1924; Estate
number on verso: *405*

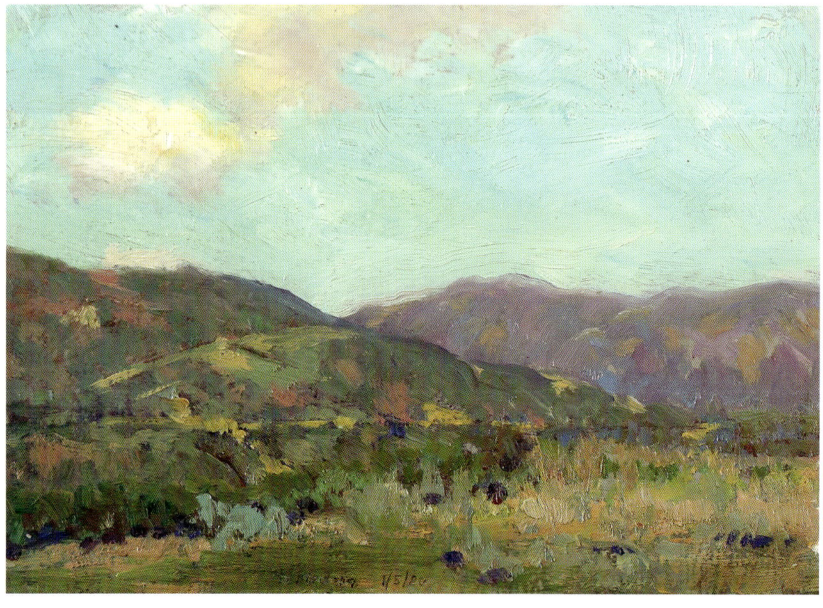

24.
Alson Skinner Clark
(1876–1949)
Arroyo Seco Mountains
(California), 1920
Oil on panel
5¾ × 8 inches
Dated and inscribed lower
center: *Medora 1/15/20*;
Dated and inscribed on
estate label on verso:
*Alson Clark, / Mountains,
California, / Dedicated 'to
Madora,' / First year here
in California, / Date 1920,
Size 5¾ x 8.*; Estate number
on verso: *465*

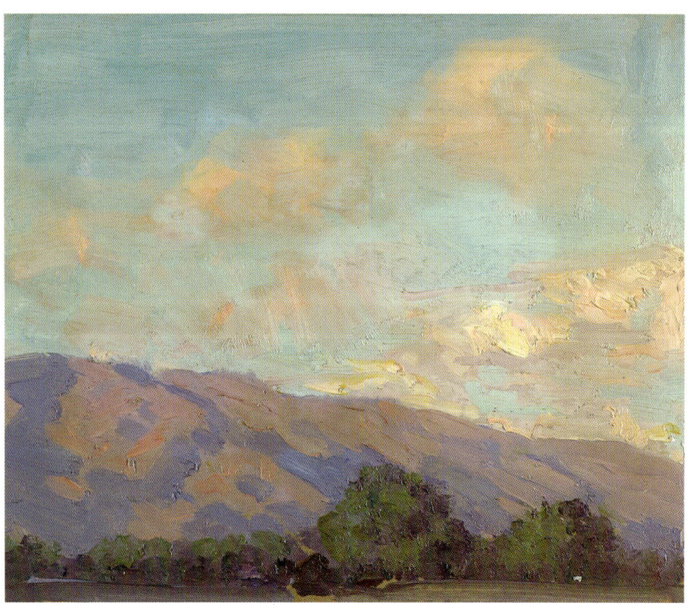

25.
Alson Skinner Clark
(1876–1949)
From the Terrace
(Pasadena, California), 1923
Oil on panel
7½ × 9½ inches
Dated on verso: *1923*
Inscribed on estate label
on verso: *From the Terrace,
Pasadena, / Alson Clark, /
1149 Wotkyns Drive, /
Pasadena, California.*;
Estate number on
verso: *387*

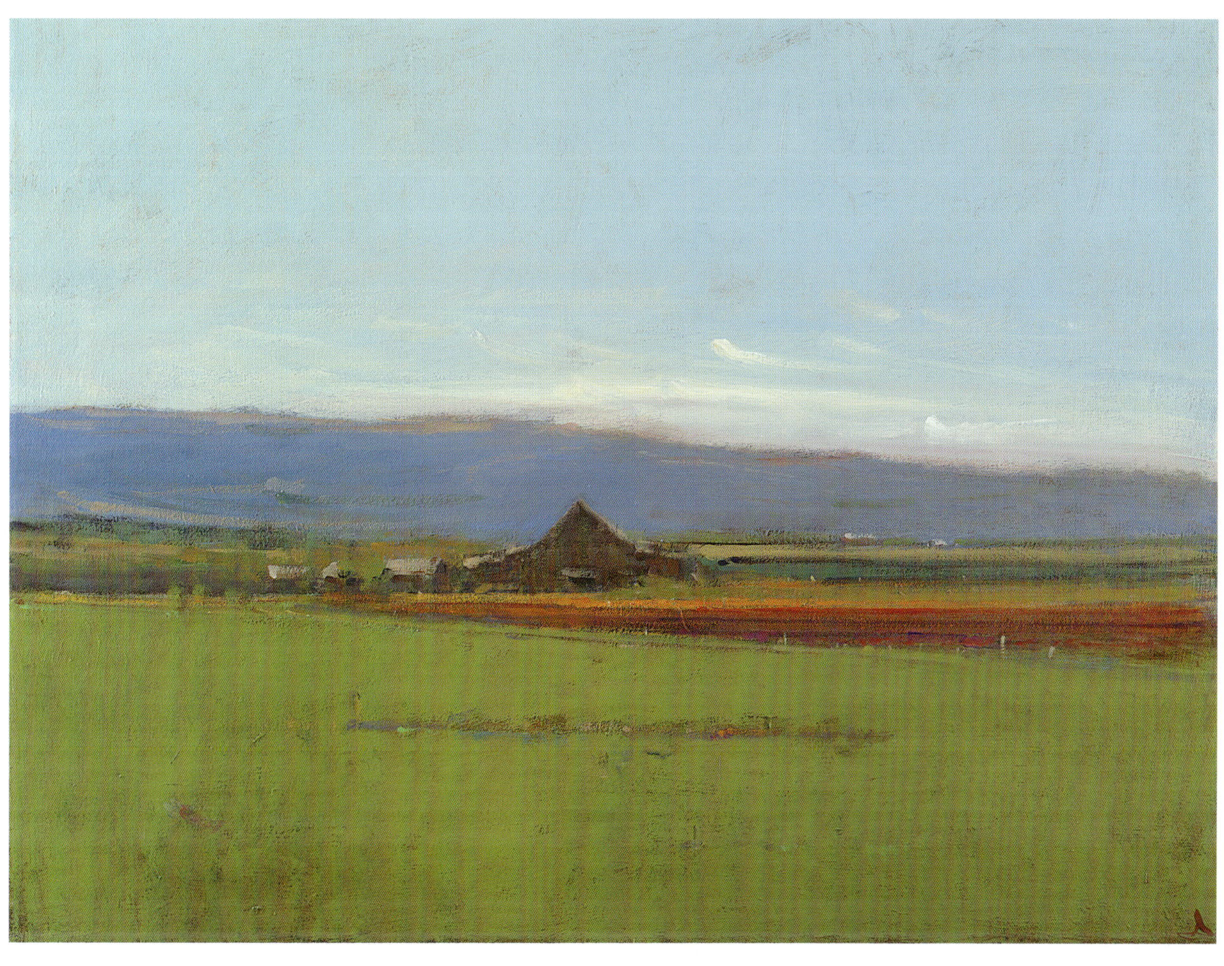

26.
Terry DeLapp (b. 1934)
Old Barn—Nipomo (California), 2003
Acrylic on canvas, 24 × 32 inches
Signed with the artist's monogrammed initials lower right:
TDL; Titled on verso: *Old Barn—Nipomo*

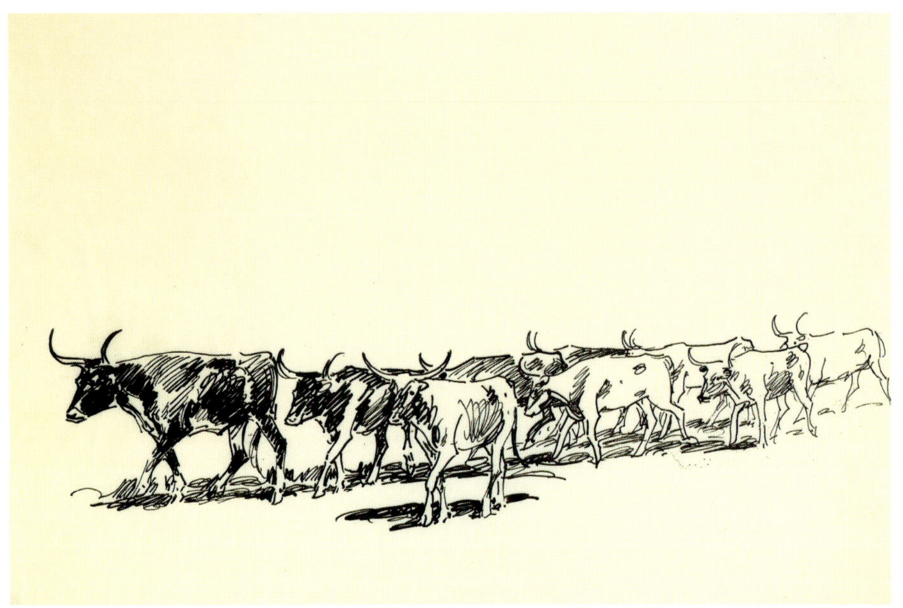

27.
Edward Borein (1872–1945)
Standing Herd, ca. 1915
Ink on paper
7½ × 12 inches

28.
Edward Borein (1872–1945)
Eight Cowboys, ca. 1915
Ink on paper
7½ × 13 inches

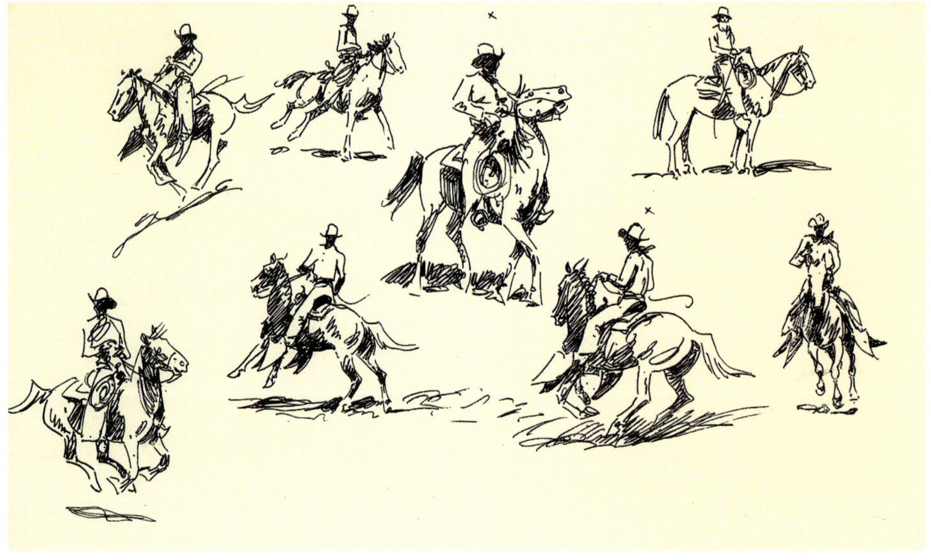

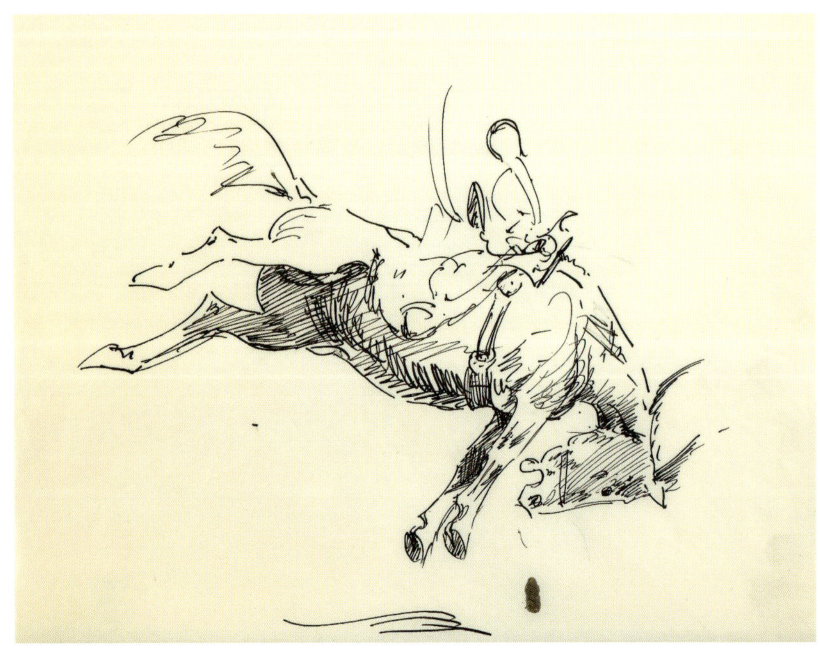

29.
Edward Borein (1872–1945)
Breakin' the Steer, ca. 1915
Ink on paper
8½ × 11 inches

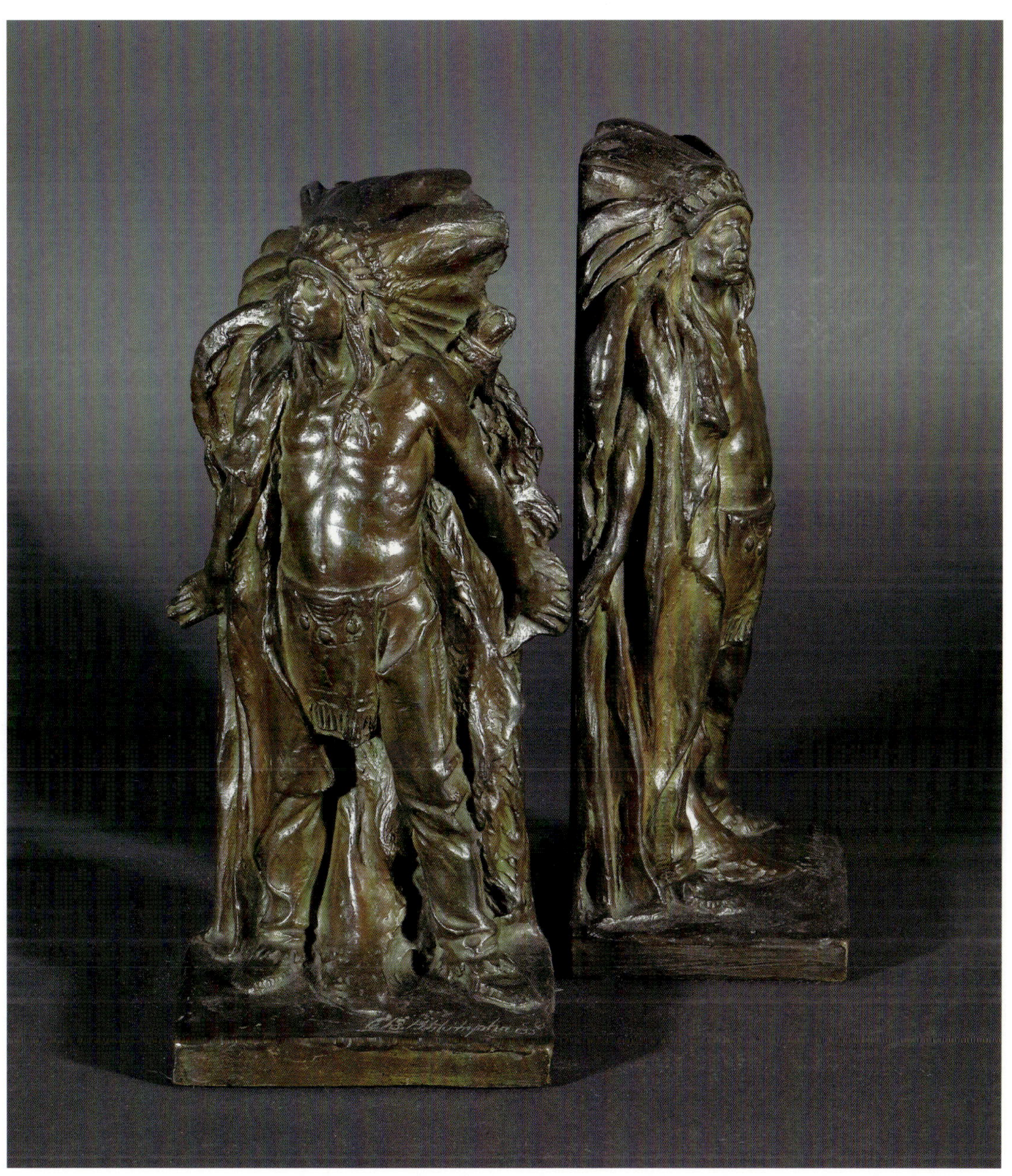

30.
Charles Harry Humphriss (1867–1964)
Indian Chief Bookends, ca. 1900–10
Bronze, height: 9½ inches
Inscribed lower right on pair: *Chs. H. Humphriss*
Inscribed on back: *Roman Bronze Works N.Y.*

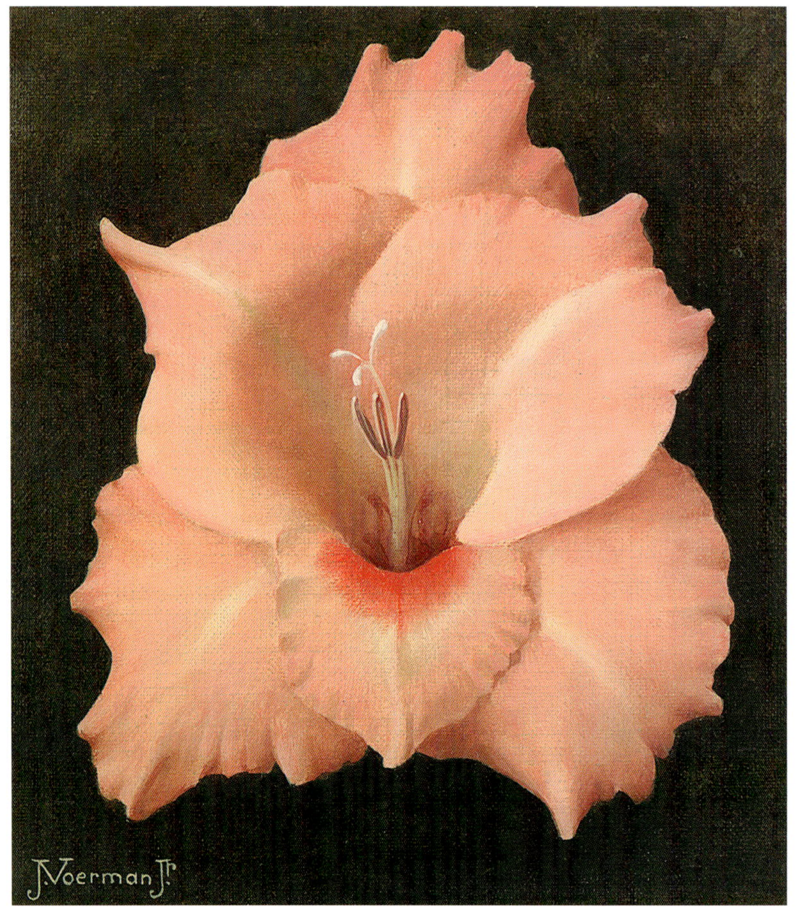

31.
Jan Voerman, Jr.
(Dutch, 1890–1976)
Gladiola (Pink), ca. 1910s
Oil on canvas mounted
on board
7¾ × 6⅞ inches
Signed lower right:
J. Voerman Jr.

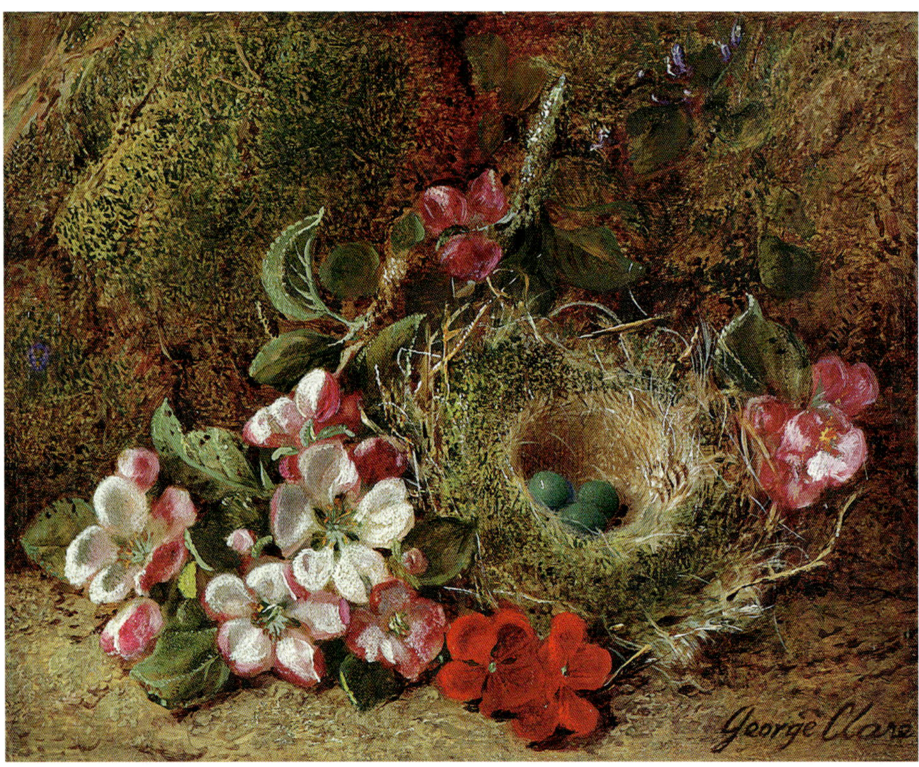

32.
George Clare
(British, 1830–1900)
*Primulas and Bird's
Nest with Eggs on a
Mossy Bank*, ca. 1860s
Oil on canvas
7 × 9 inches
Signed lower right:
George Clare

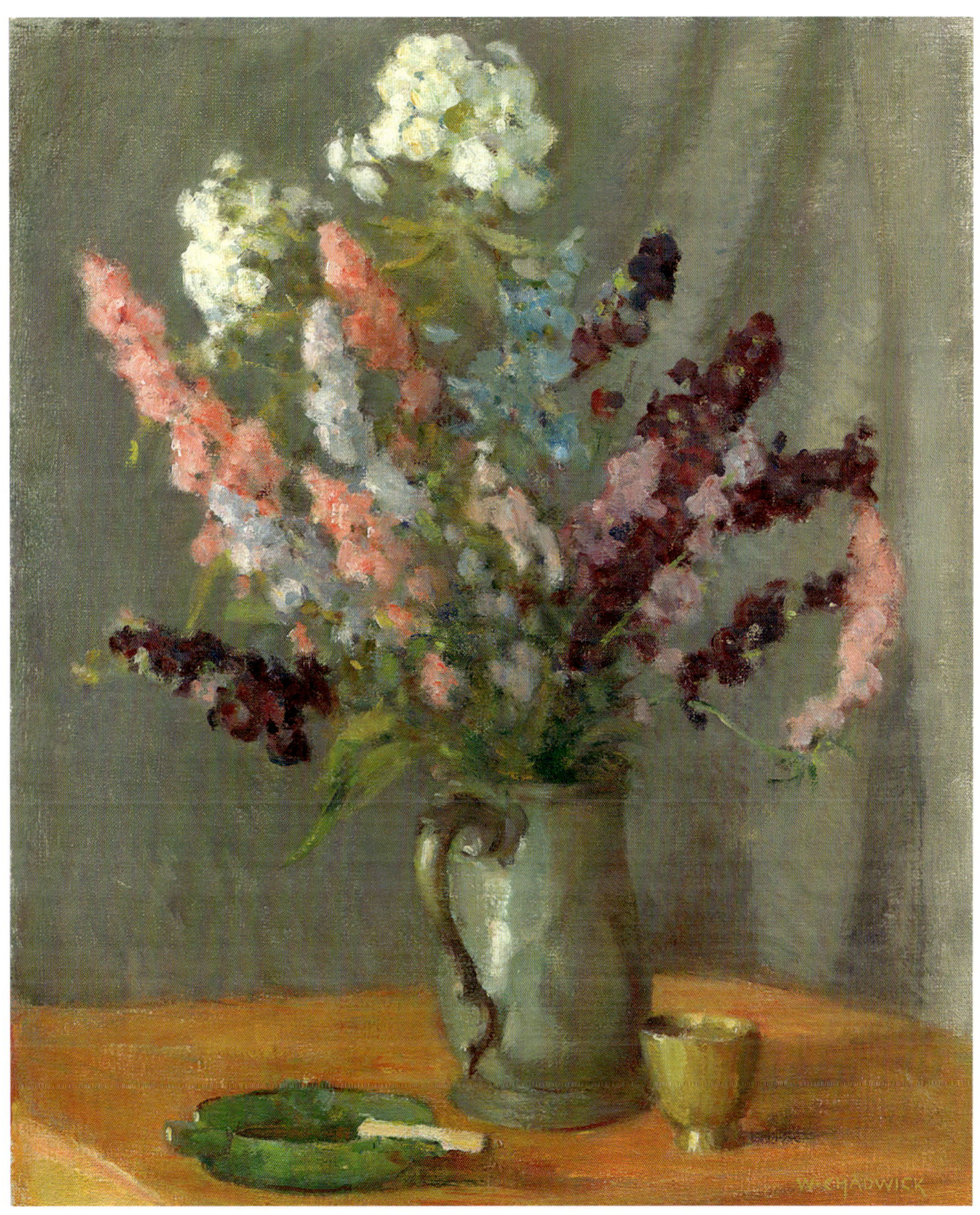

33.
William Chadwick (1879–1962)
A Pewter Mug with Delphiniums, ca. 1910s
Oil on canvas, 24 × 20 inches
Signed lower right: *W. Chadwick*

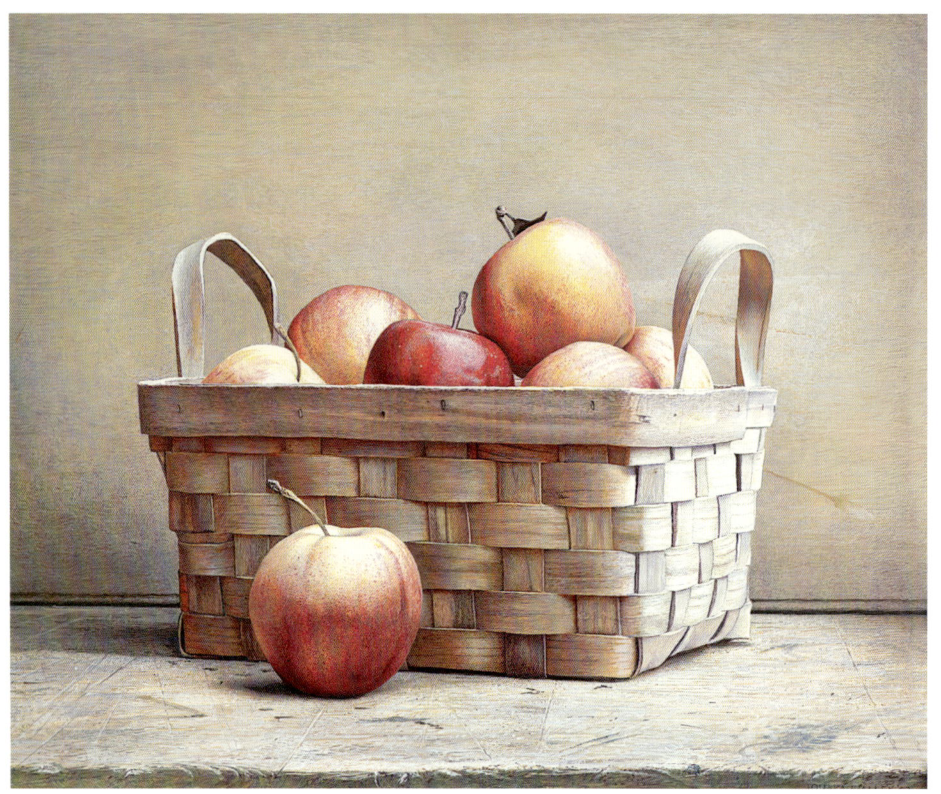

34.
John Whalley (b. 1954)
Basket of Apples, 2003
Egg tempera on panel
14 × 17 inches
Signed and dated lower
right: *John Whalley 03*

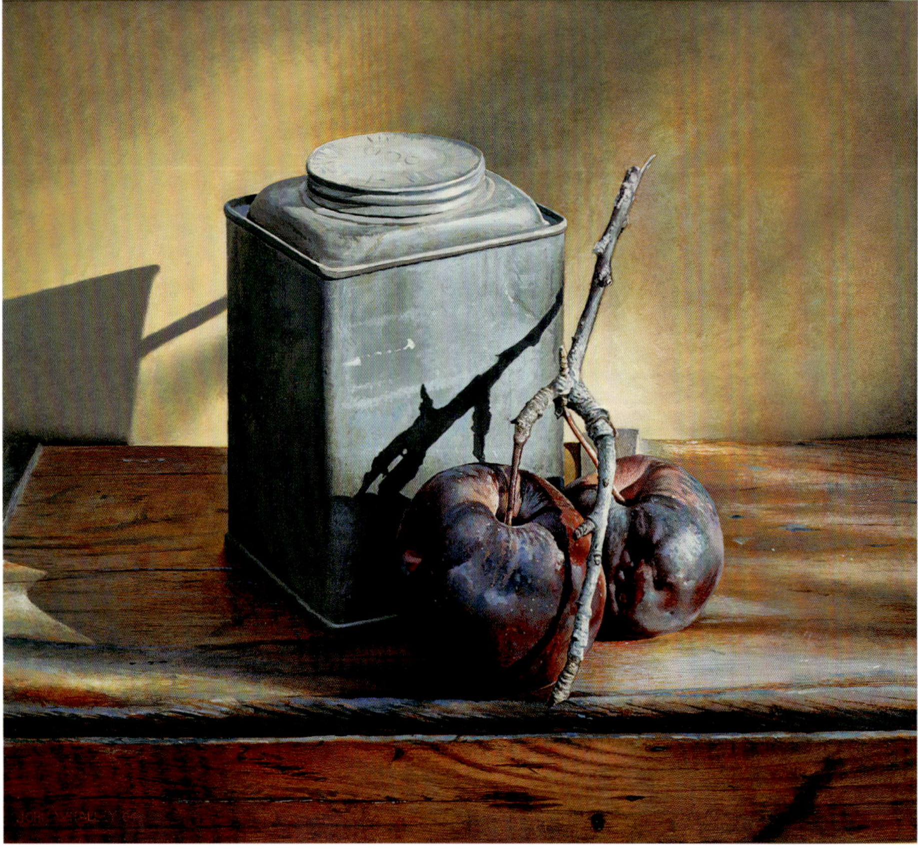

35.
John Whalley (b. 1954)
Wild Apples, 2004
Oil on panel
15¼ × 17½ inches
Signed and dated lower
left: *John Whalley 04*

36.
Etsuo Shimizu
(Japanese, b. 1953)
Siesta, ca. 1990s
Oil on canvas
9½ × 13 inches
Signed lower left: [illeg.]

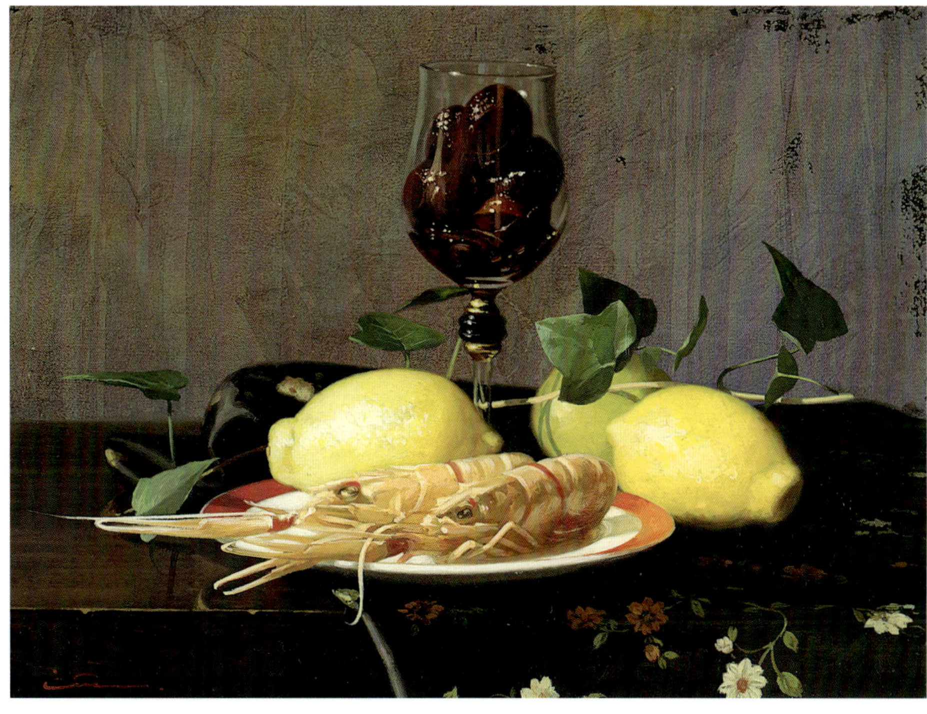

37.
Yin Yong Chun (b. 1958)
Pumpkin in a Bowl, 2005
Oil on canvas
24 × 24 inches
Signed and dated lower
right: *Yin Yong Chun 05*

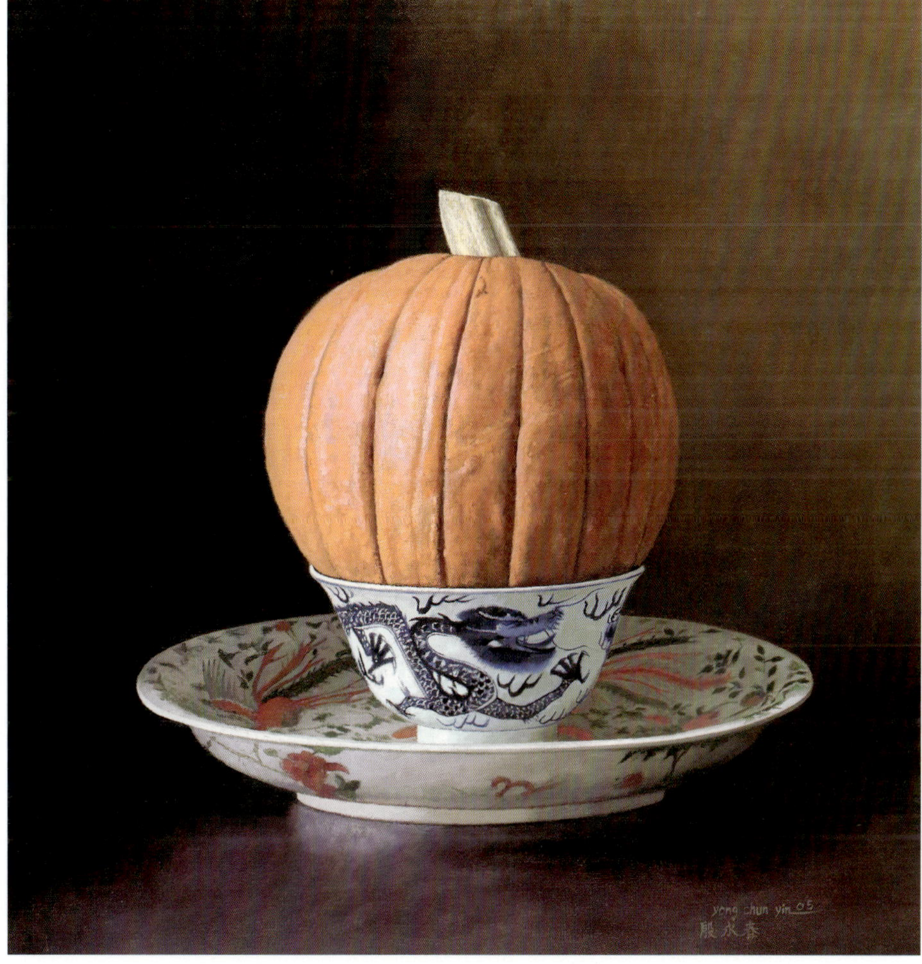

38.
Annie Gooding Sykes
(1855–1931)
Backyard Flower Garden
(possibly Gloucester,
Massachusetts), ca. 1910
Watercolor on paper
19¾ × 14 inches
Signed lower right:
A G Sykes

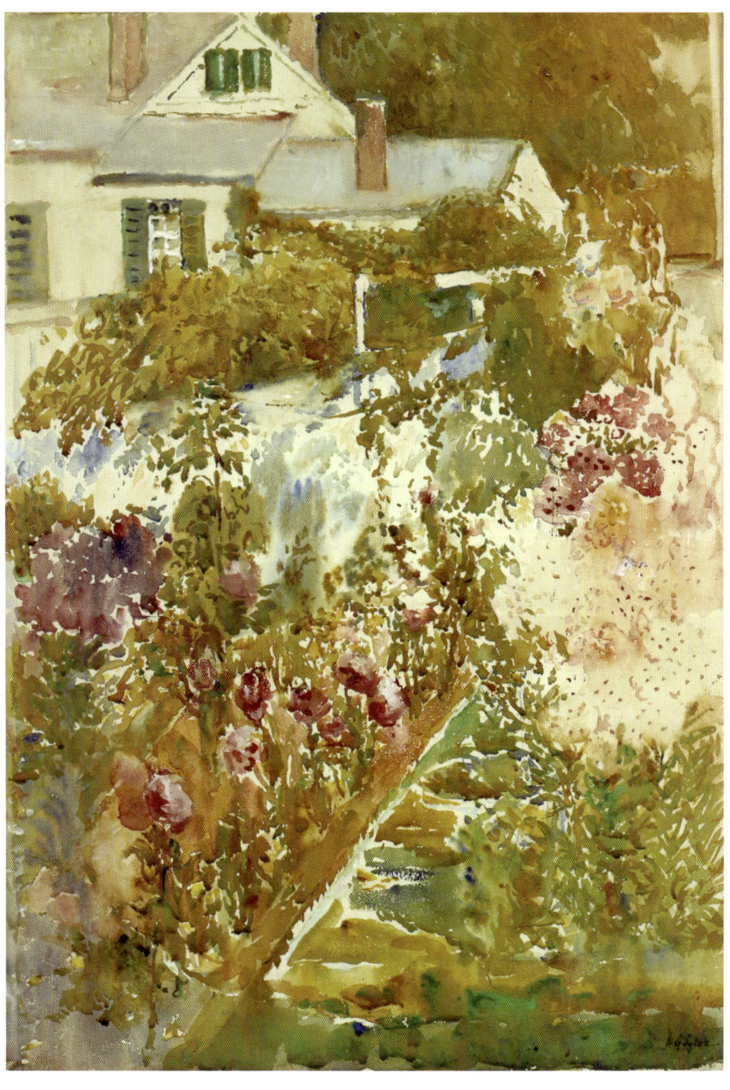

39.
Frances Foy (1890–1963)
Floral Still Life, 1930
Watercolor on paper
12½ × 12 inches
Signed and dated lower
right: *Frances Foy 1930*

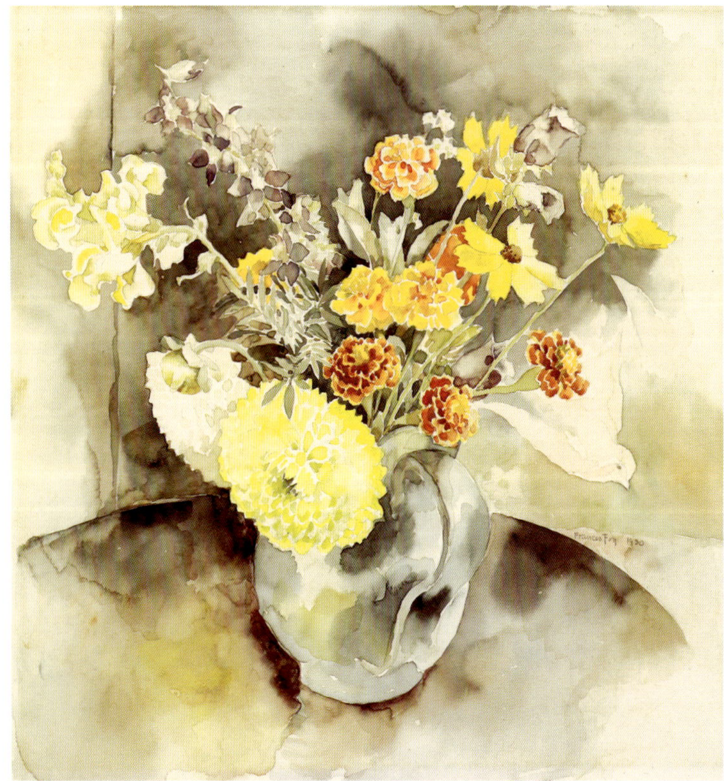

40.
Annie Gooding Sykes
(1855–1931)
Sunny Courtyard (possibly
Plymouth, Massachusetts),
ca. 1920s
Watercolor on paper
13 × 21¾ inches
Signed lower left:
A. G. Sykes

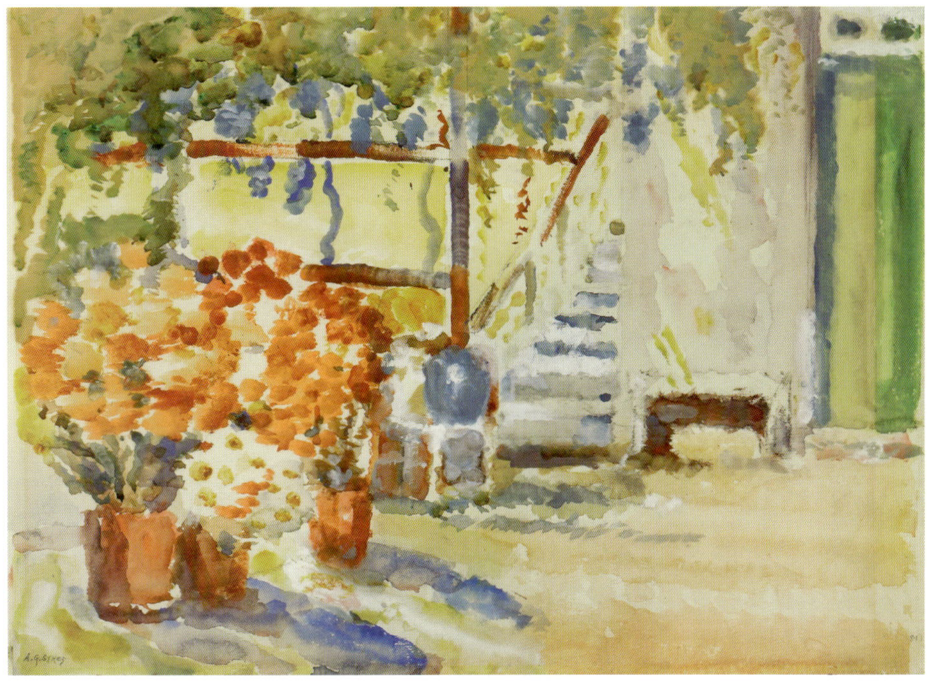

41.
Frederick Frieseke
(1874–1939)
Interior, Holland, 1898
Watercolor on paper
12 × 9¾ inches
Signed, dated, and
inscribed lower left:
F. C. Frieseke / Holland 98.

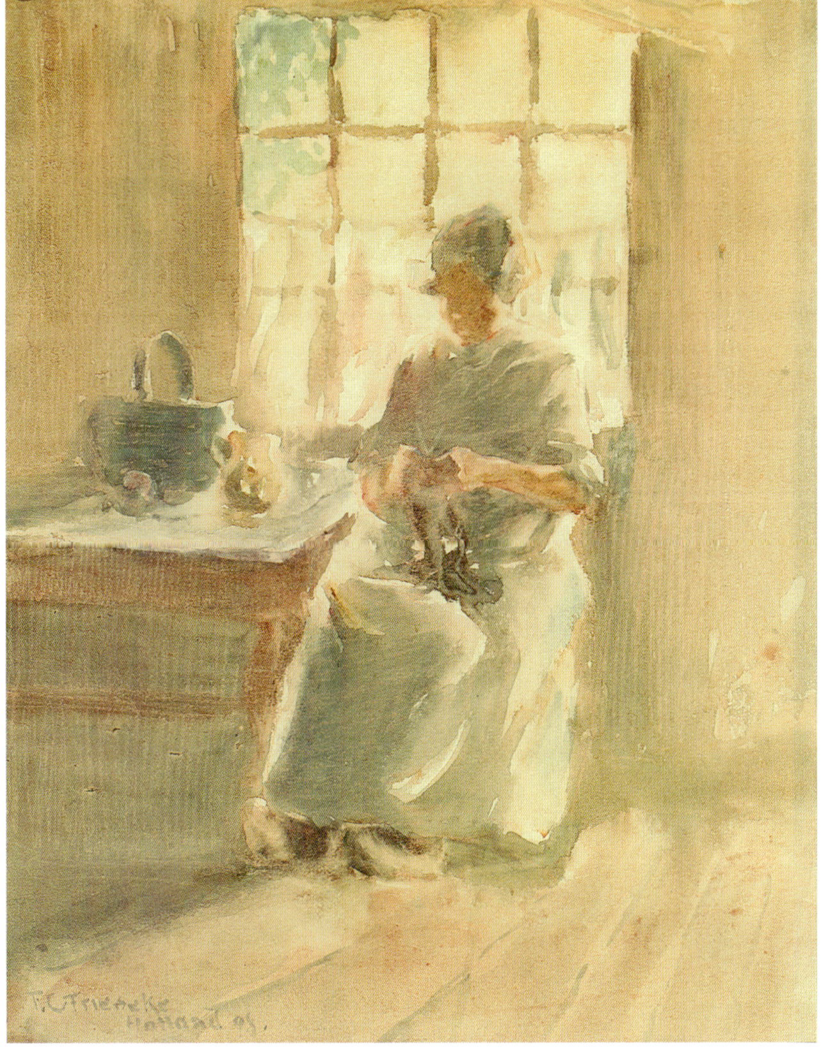

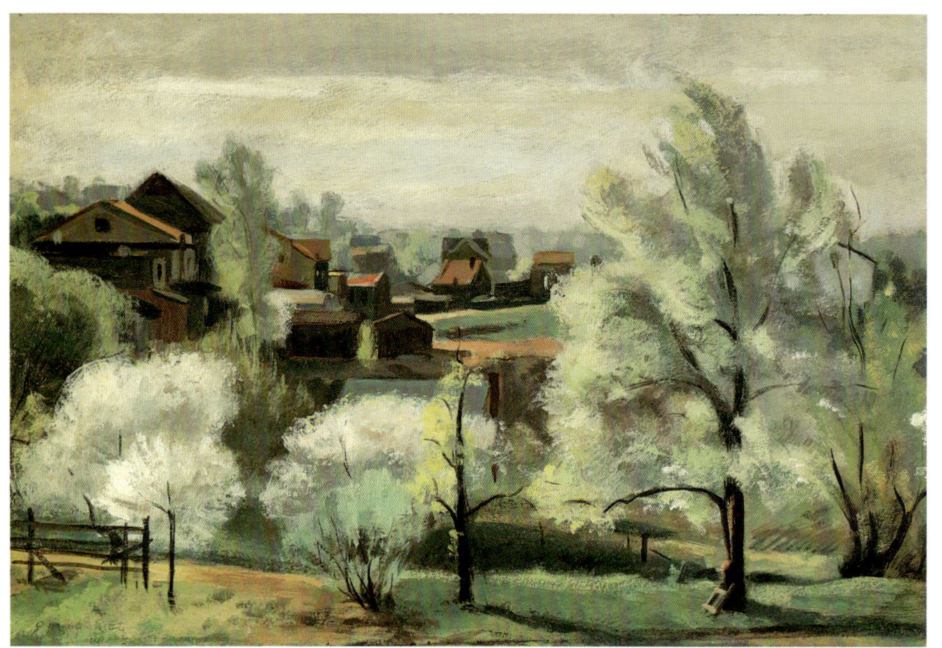

42.
Giovanni Martino
(1908–1998)
Study for Spring
Blossoms (Manayunk,
Pennsylvania), ca. 1930s
Oil on panel
12 × 18 inches
Signed lower left: *Giovanni
Martino*; Inscribed on
verso: *Study for "Spring
Blossoms" / Giovanni
Martino. N.A.*; Inscribed
on estate label on verso:
*235 Study for / 12" x 18"
Spring Blossoms*
Small sketch on verso

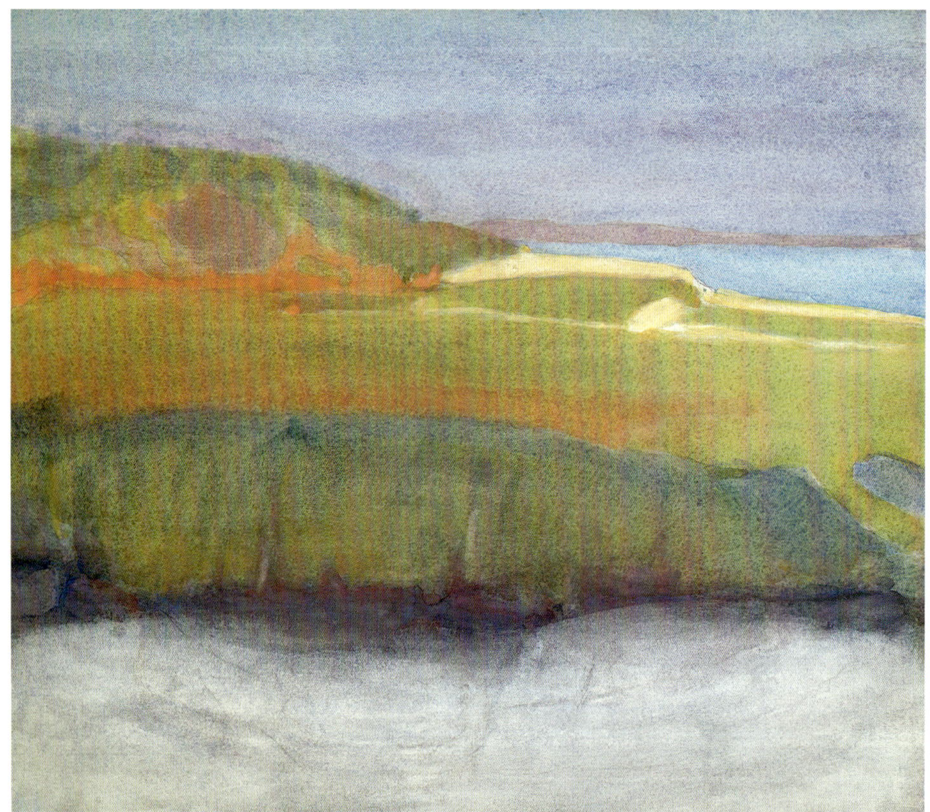

43.
**Margaret Jordan
Patterson** (1867–1950)
Cape Cod Landscape,
ca. 1910s
Watercolor on board
15 × 18 inches

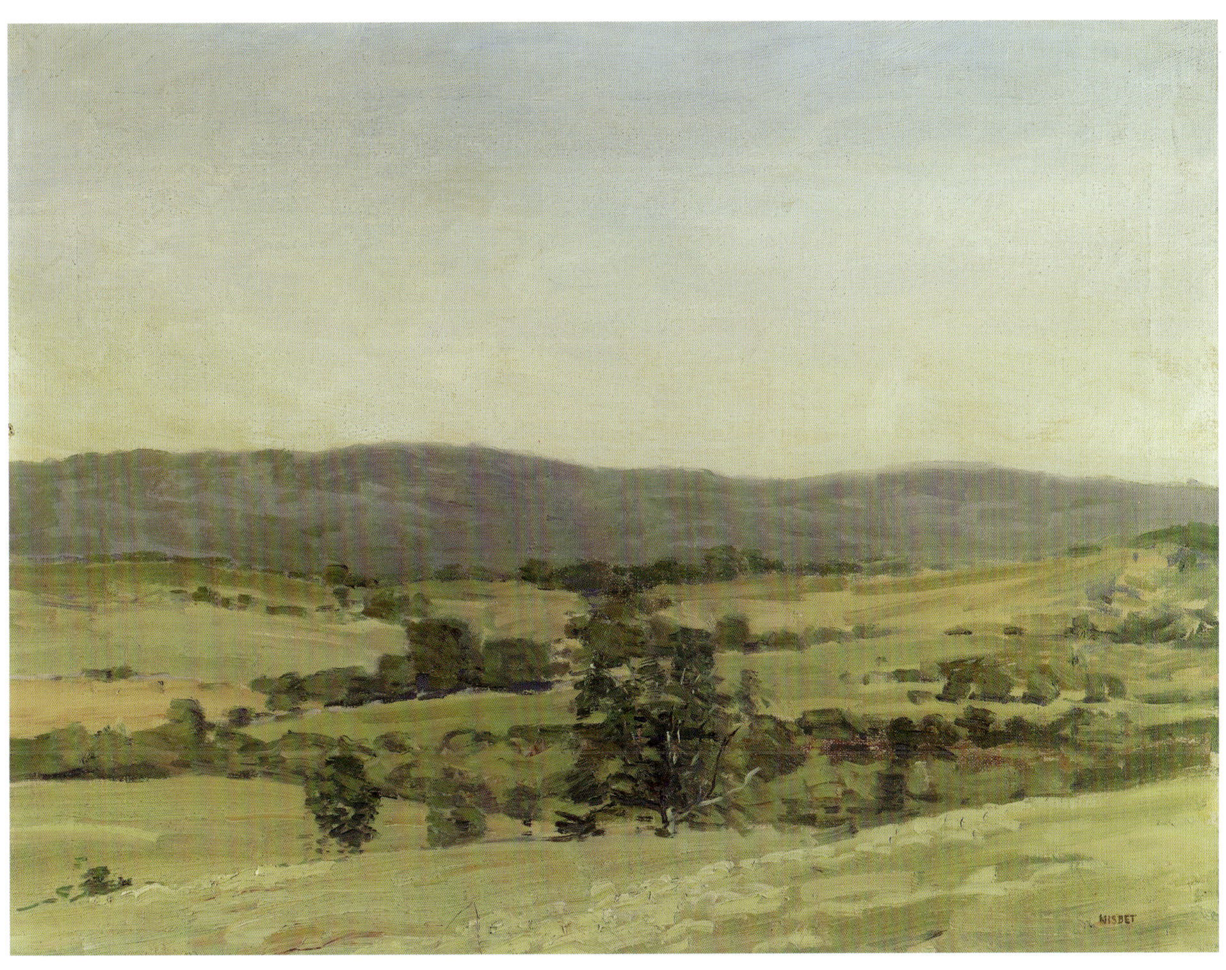

44.
Robert H. Nisbet (1879–1961)
Rolling Meadows (near Kent, Connecticut), ca. 1910s
Oil on canvas, 18⅛ × 24¼ inches
Signed lower right: *Nisbet*

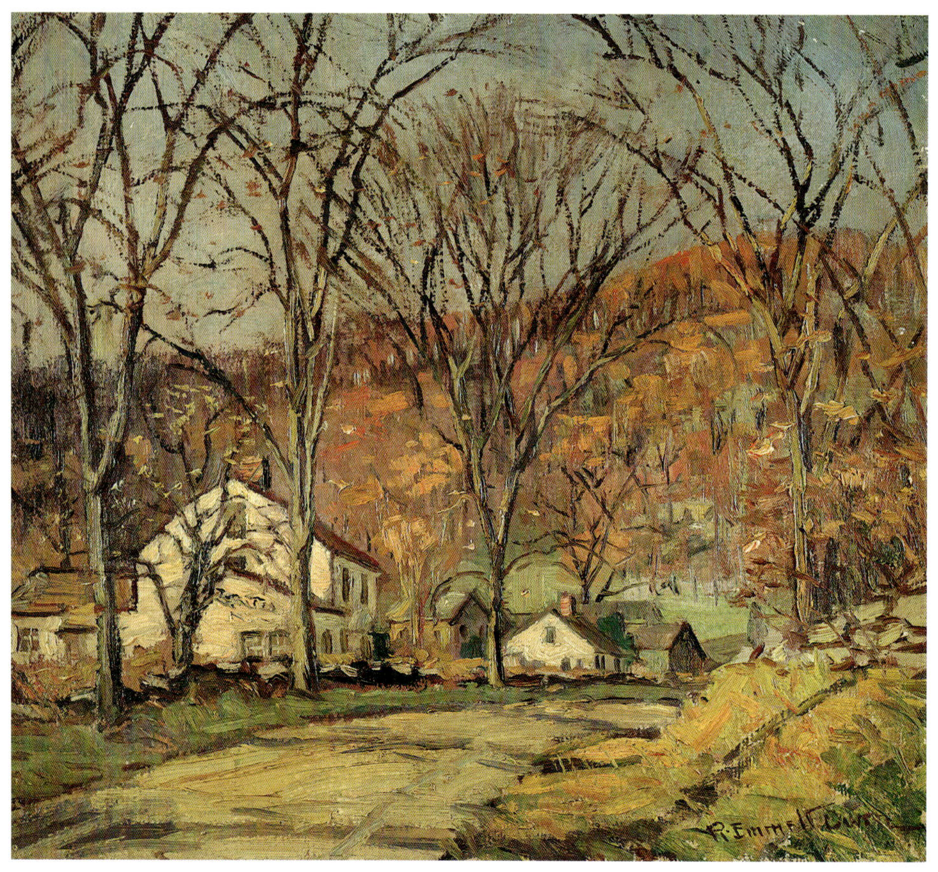

45.
Robert Emmett Owen
(1878–1957)
Study for The Road to
Sherman (New
Hampshire), ca. 1920s–30s
Oil on canvas
16½ × 20⅛ inches
Signed lower right:
R. Emmett Owen

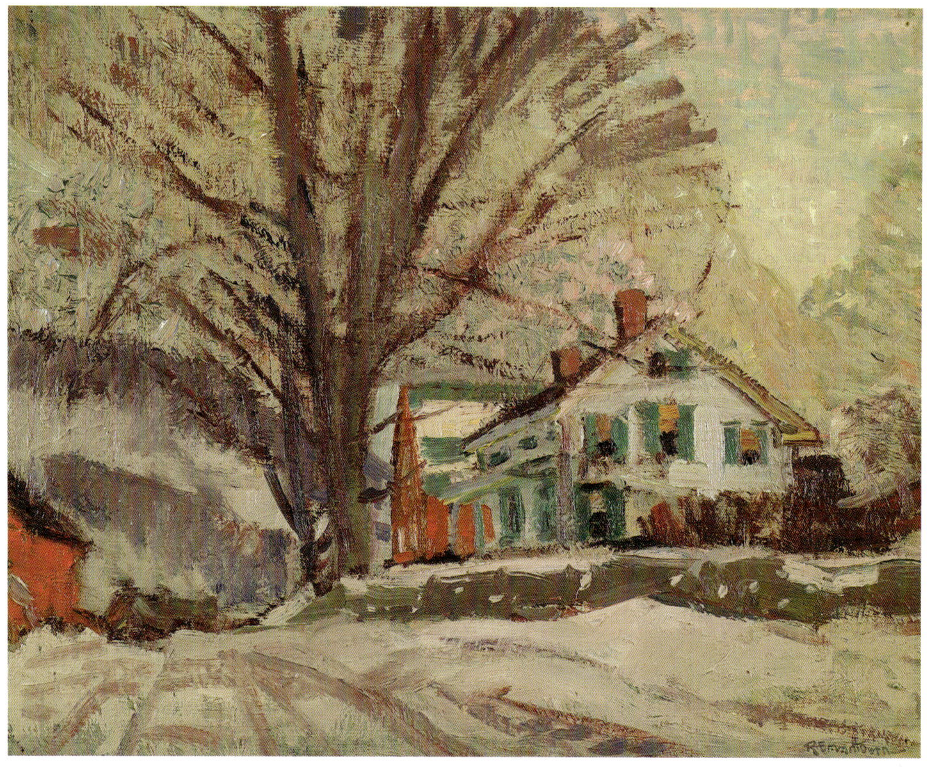

46.
Robert Emmett Owen
(1878–1957)
House and Trees,
ca. 1920s–30s
Oil on canvas
18 × 20 inches
Signed lower right:
R. Emmett Owen

47.
Robert Emmett Owen
(1878–1957)
*West Plymouth, New
Hampshire,* ca. 1920s–30s
Oil on canvas
16 × 20 inches
Inscribed on verso: *West
Plymouth, New Hampshire*

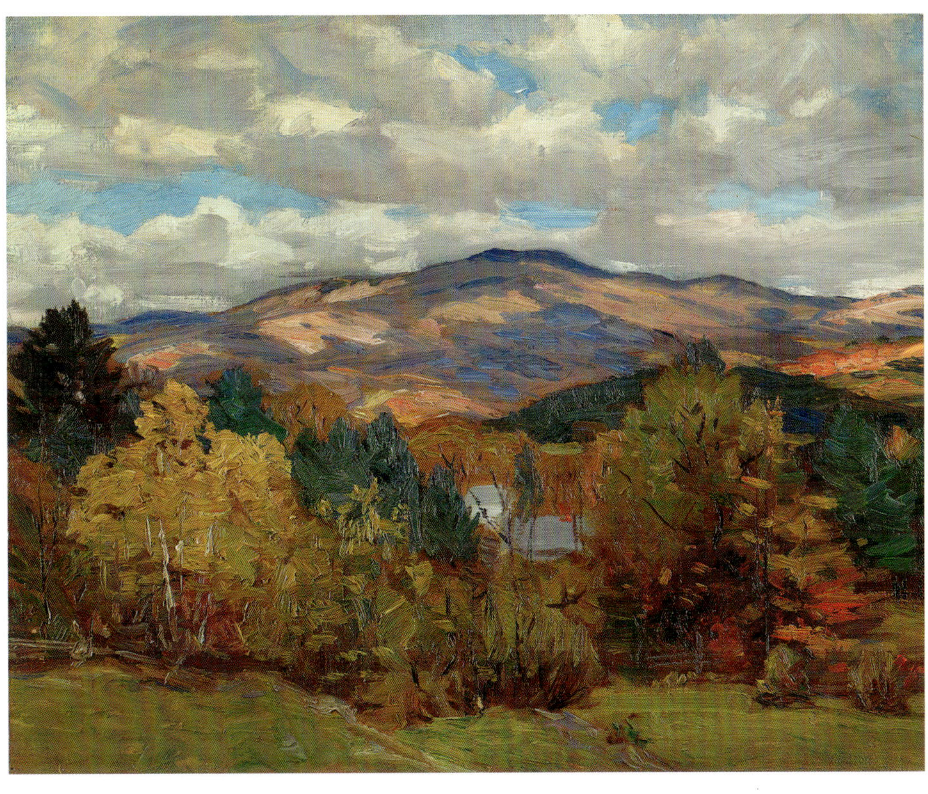

48.
Robert Emmett Owen
(1878–1957)
*Smith Covered Bridge at
North Plymouth, New
Hampshire,* ca. 1920s–30s
Oil on canvas
20 × 24 inches
Signed lower right:
R. Emmett Owen

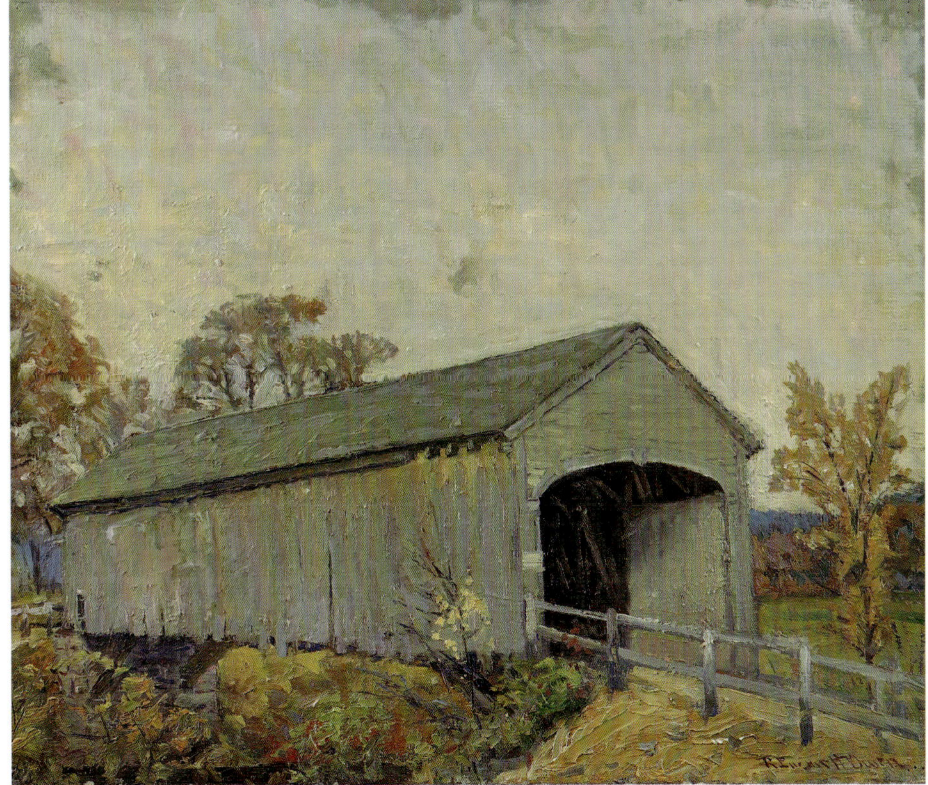

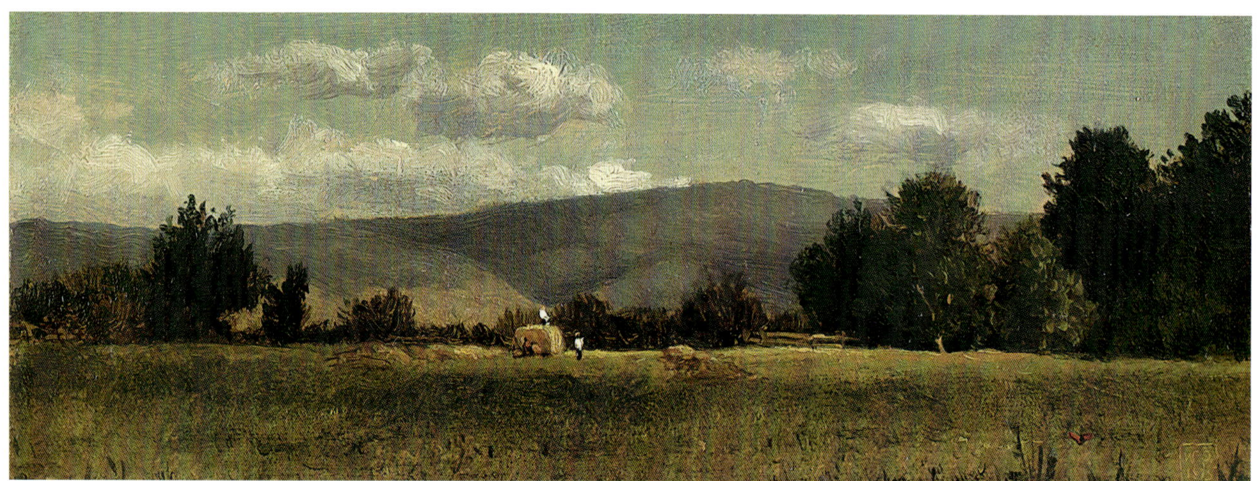

49.
Walter Launt Palmer (1854–1932)
Landscape, 1875
oil on paper mounted on canvas mounted on panel
4½ × 11 inches. Signed with the artist's monogrammed
initials and dated lower right: *W. P. / 1875*

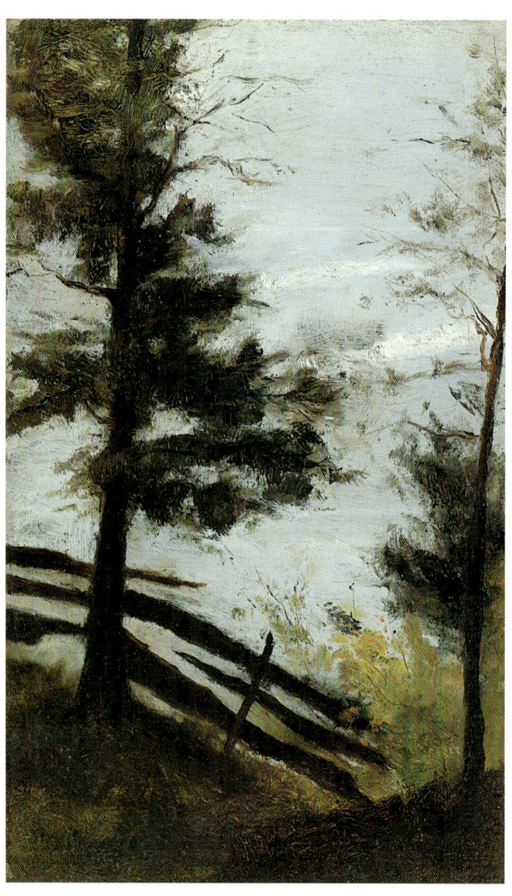

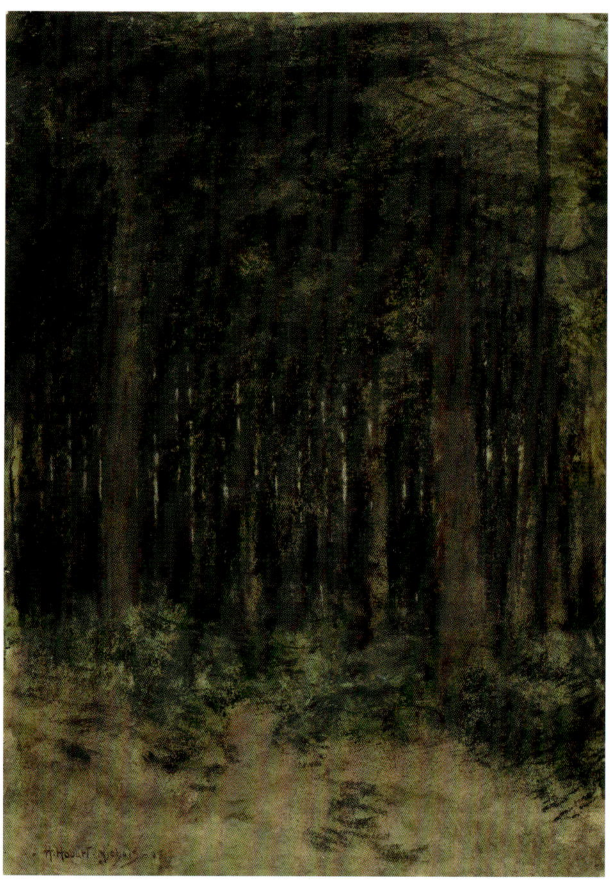

51.
Henry Hobart Nichols (1869–1962)
Twilight in the Pines, 1905
Pastel on paper
20½ × 14⅝ inches
Signed and dated lower left: *H. Hobart Nichols, 05*

50.
Charles Harold Davis (1856–1933)
Trees in Landscape, ca. 1890s
Oil on board
10¼ × 6½ inches

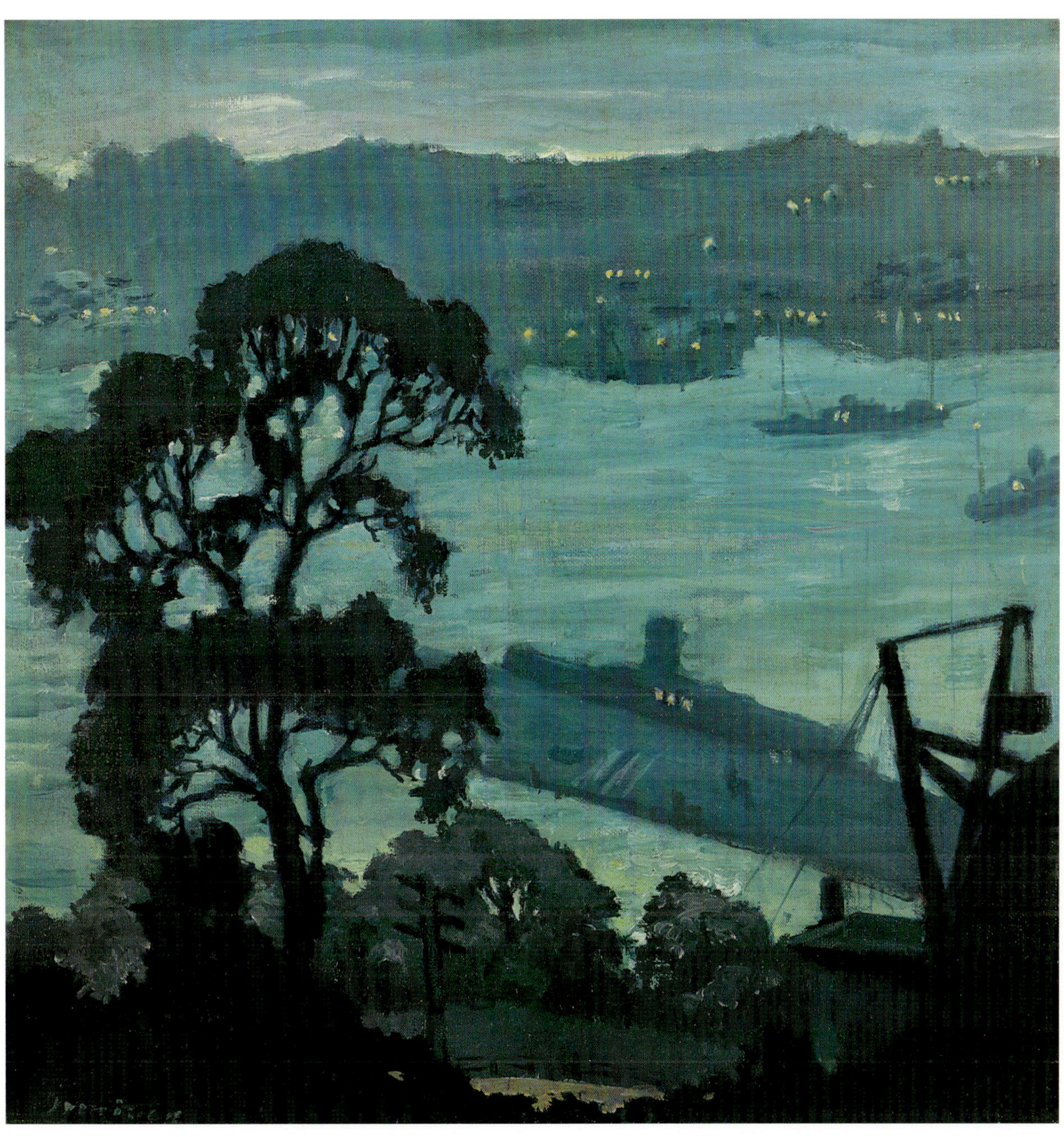

52.
MacGregor Ormiston (20th century)
River at Night, ca. 1920s
Oil on canvas
16 × 16 inches
Signed lower left: *Ormiston*

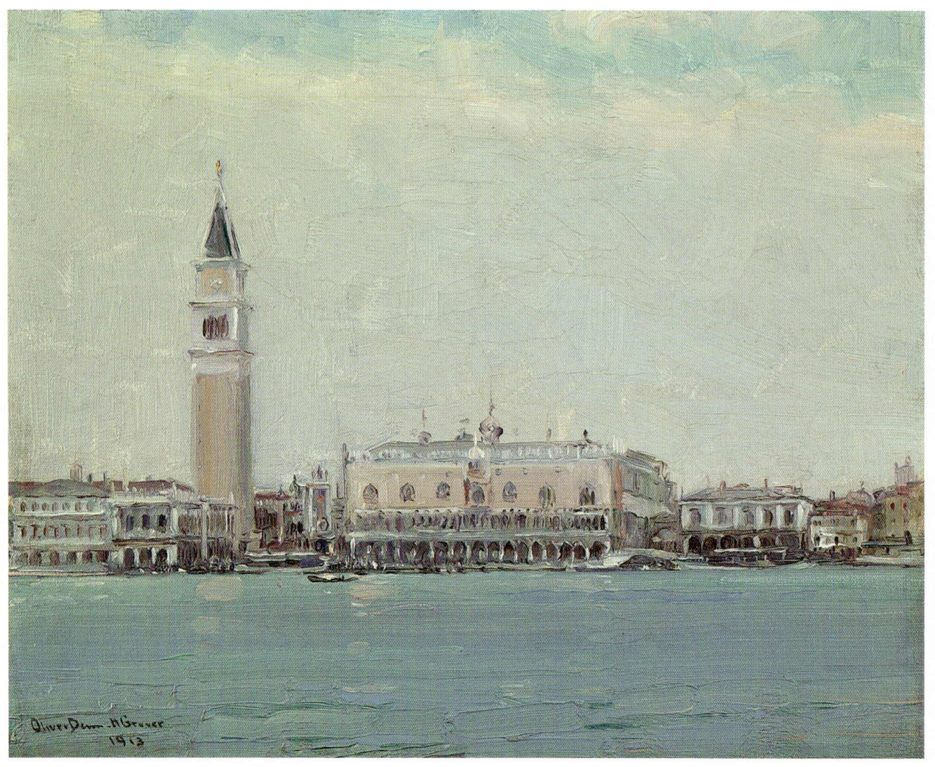

53.
Oliver Dennett Grover
(1861–1927)
*Venice from the Steps of
San Giorgio Maggiore,* 1913
Oil on canvas
11 × 15 inches
Signed and dated lower
left: *Oliver Denn. M Grover
/ 1913*; Signed and inscribed
by artist on label on verso:
*#30. / From the steps / of
San Gior / Grover*

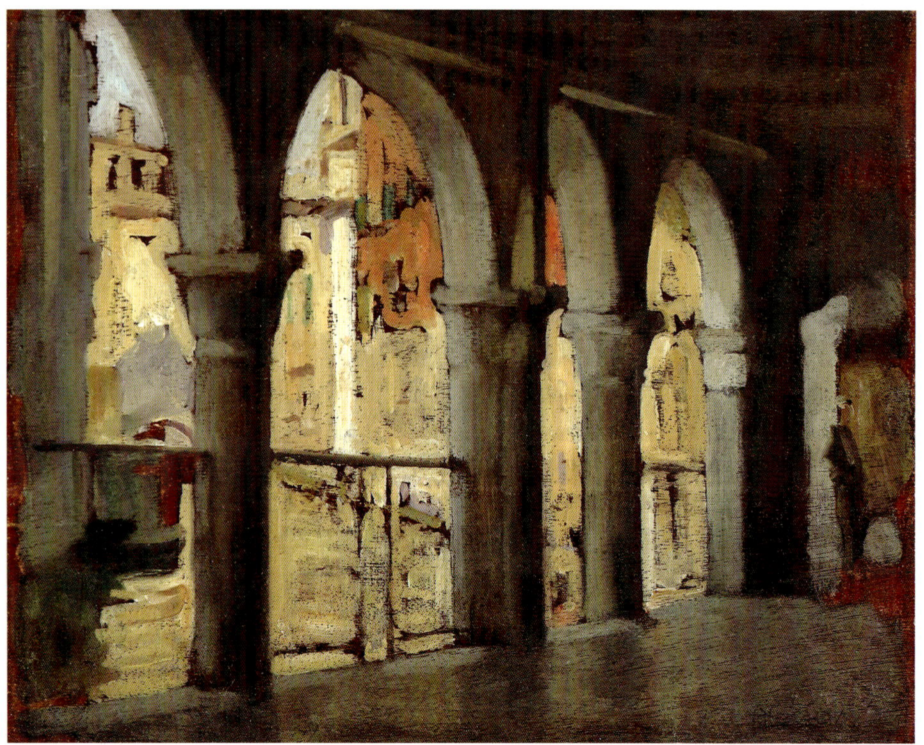

54.
Alson Skinner Clark
(1876–1949)
Arcade in Venice, 1903
Oil on panel
7½ × 9½ inches
Signed lower right: *Alson
Clark*; Dated and inscribed
on estate label on verso:
*Alson Clark. / Arcade in
Venice, painted / on a trip
to Italy in the / spring of
1903 / size 9½ x 7½.;* Estate
number on verso: *703*

55.
Frank Myers Boggs
(1855–1926)
The Basin at Rouen,
ca. 1900
Watercolor and charcoal
on paper
9½ × 13½ inches
Signed and inscribed lower
left: *Frank—Boggs/Rouen*

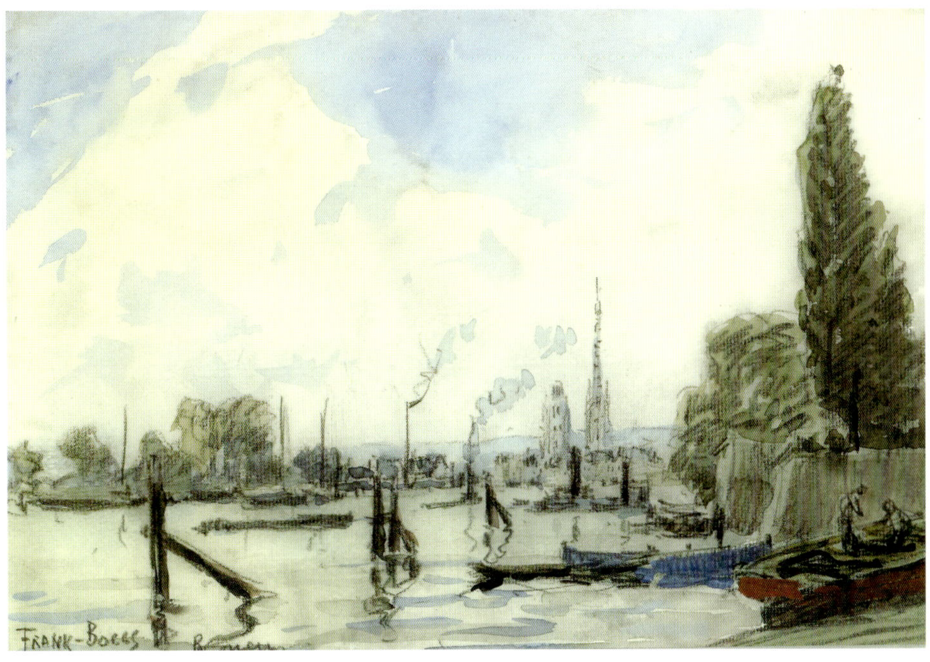

56.
Colin Campbell Cooper
(1856–1937)
Stresa (Italy), 1924
Gouache on paper
4¾ × 7¼ inches
Signed, dated, and
inscribed lower left:
C. / Stresa. / June 25th / 29

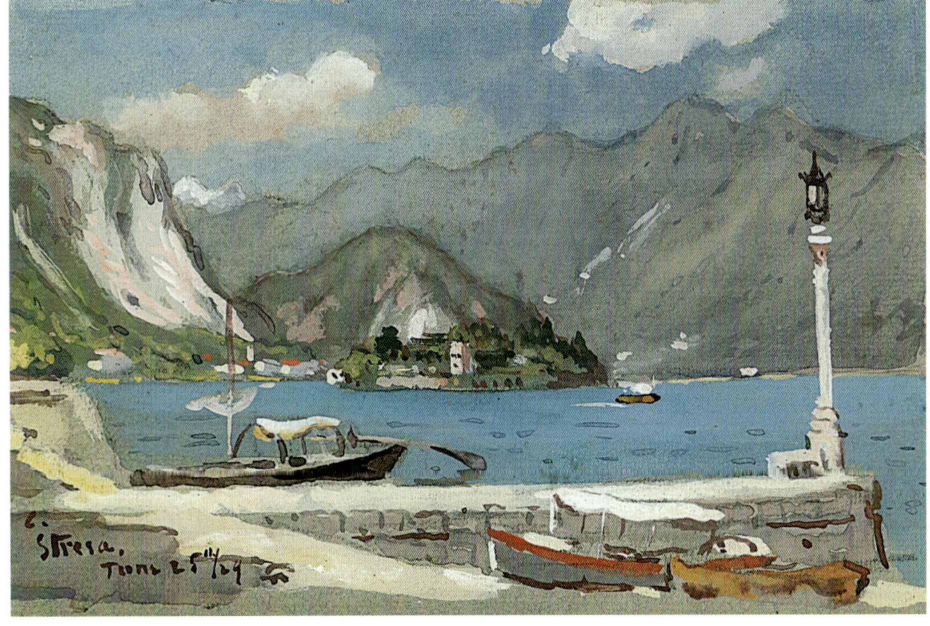

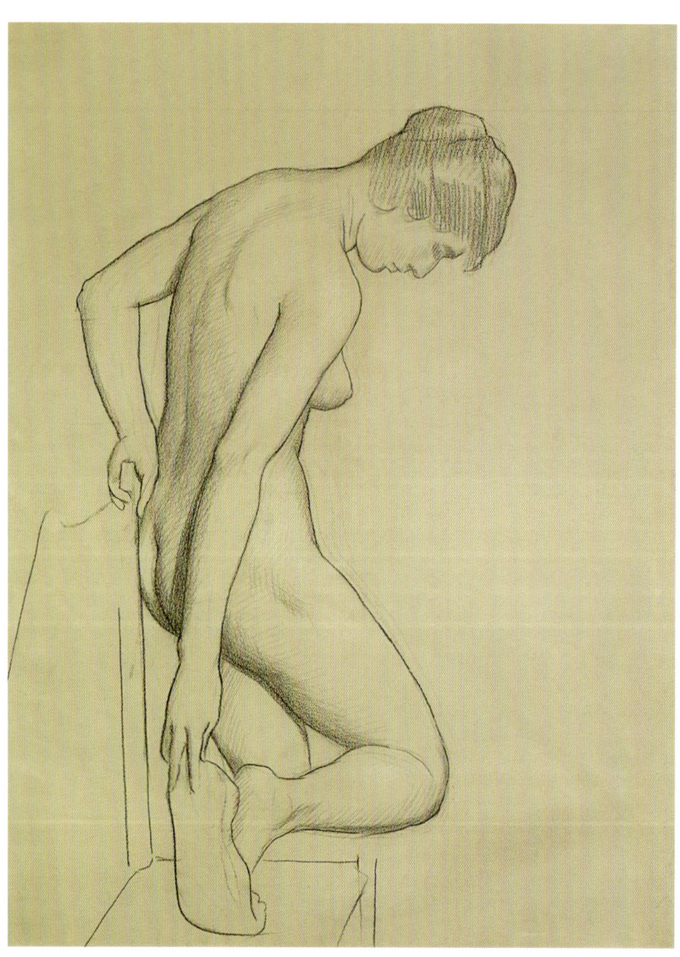

57.
William McGregor Paxton
(1869–1941)
After the Bath, ca. 1920
Charcoal on paper
23½ × 18 inches
Inscribed on a letter on
verso: *To whom it may
concern: / I inherited this /
drawing by Paxton from /
my God-father Ives
Gammell. / It was given to
him by Paxton's widow.
Elizabeth Ives Hunter*

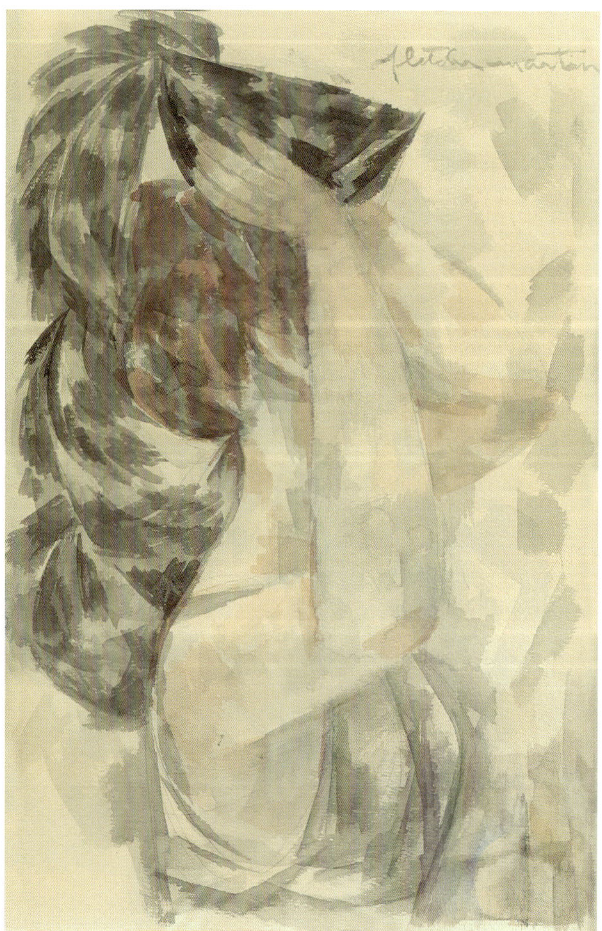

58.
Fletcher Martin
(1904–1979)
Fitting the Hat, ca. 1940s
Watercolor on paper
20½ × 14¼ inches
Signed upper right:
Fletcher Martin

59.
Albert Sterner (1863–1946)
Marie, 1921
Sanguine on paper
17 × 10½ inches
Signed and dated lower
left: *Albert Sterner 1921*
Signed, stamped, and
inscribed by artist on label
on verso: *Albert Sterner /
Marie Seated / Sanguine
Drawing*

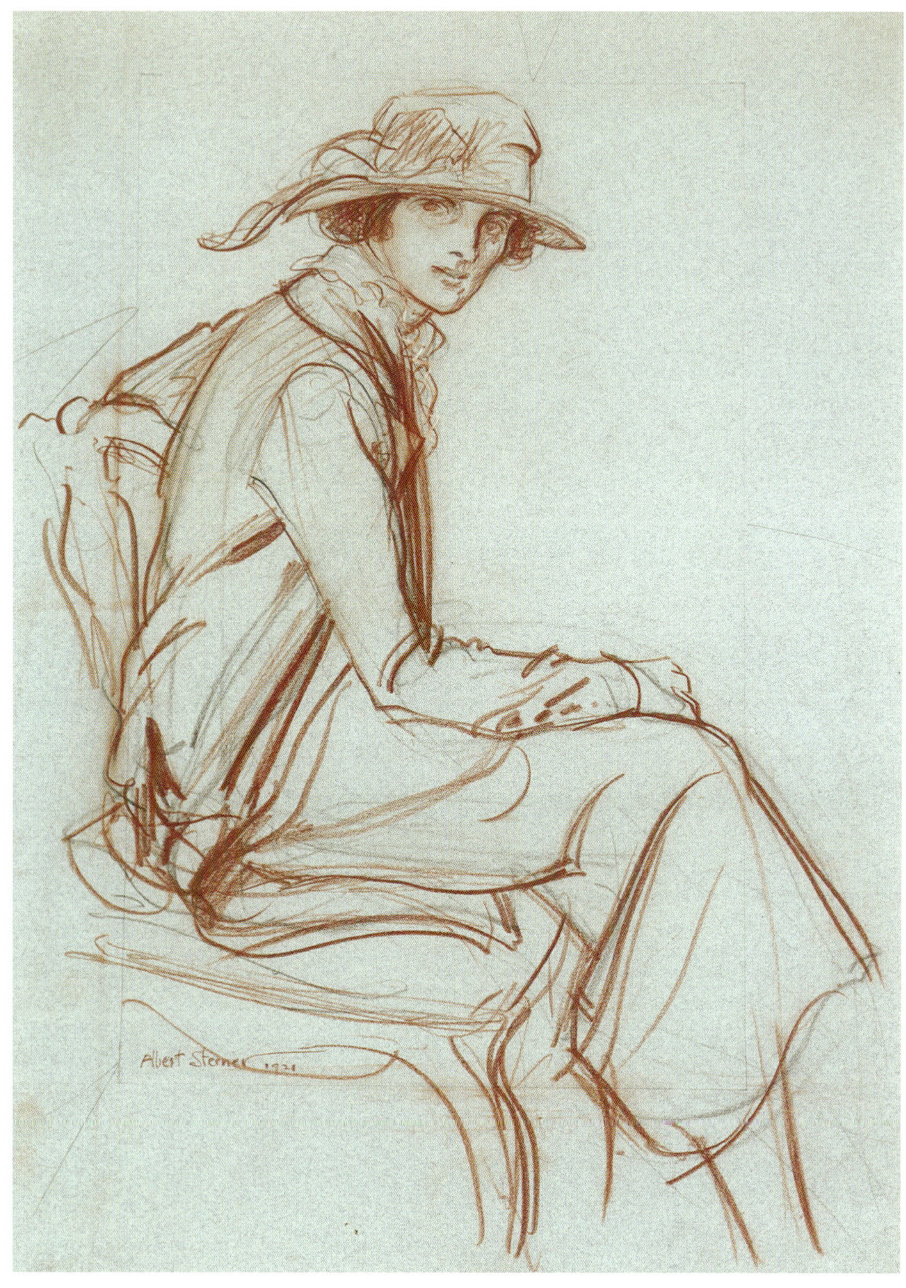

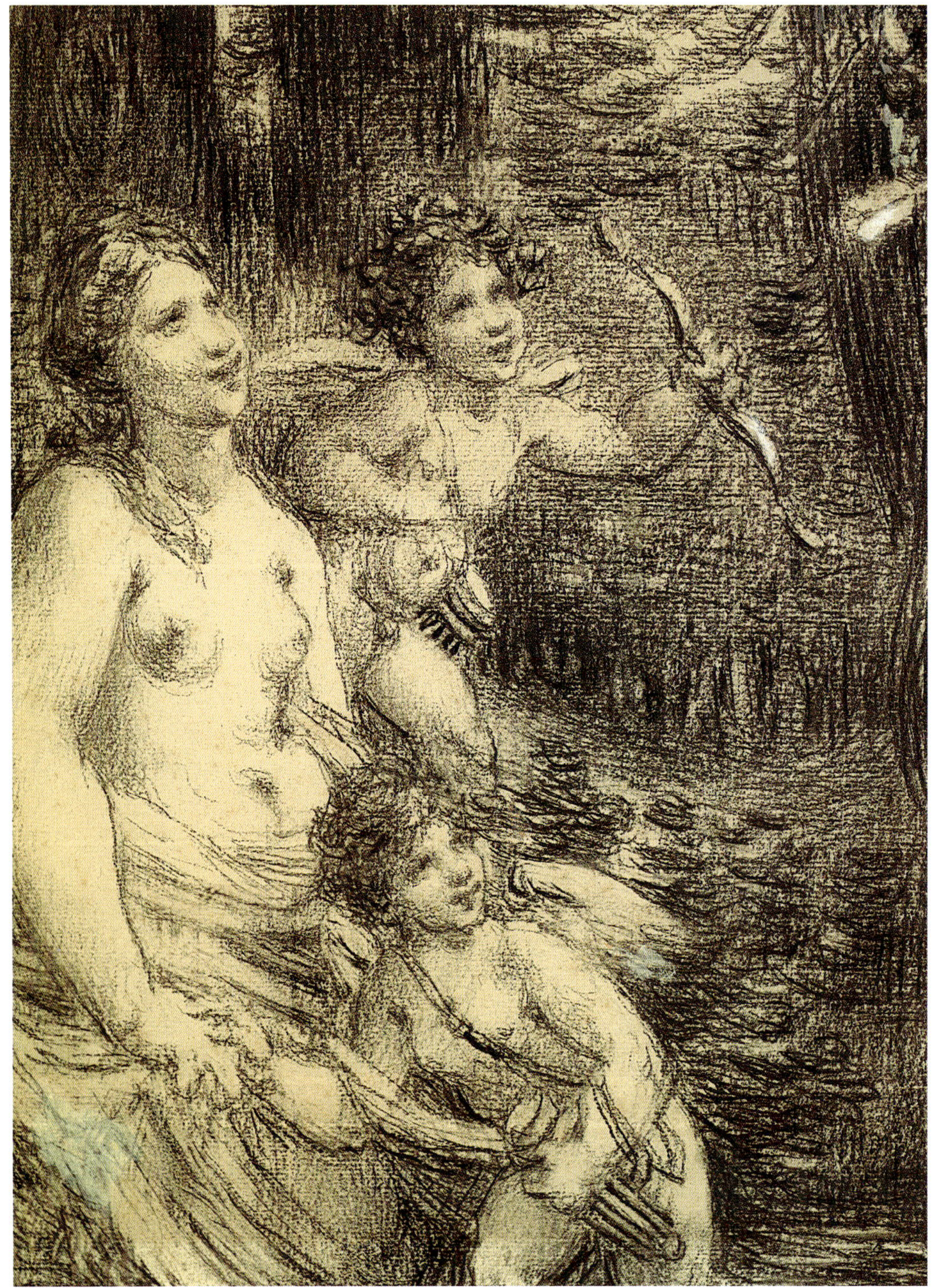

60.
William Perkins Babcock
(1826–1899)
*Venus and Cupids in
a Forest,* ca. 1870s
Charcoal on paper
12½ × 9¼ inches

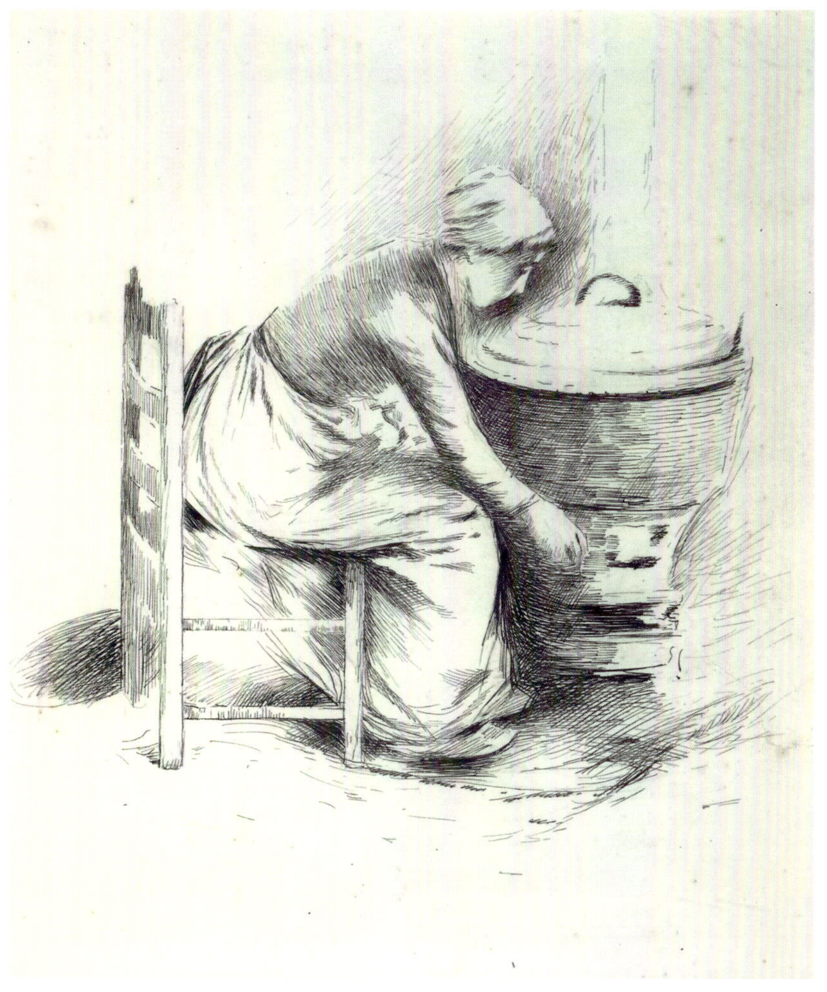

61.
Theodore Robinson
(1852–1896)
*Woman at a Hearth,
Normandy,* ca. 1875–79
Ink on paper laid on paper
14½ × 13 inches
Signed and inscribed lower
left: *Normandy Interior /
Theo. Robinson.*

62.
William Glackens
(1870–1938)
*On Beach Avenue, Atlantic
City* (New Jersey), ca. 1900s
Pen, ink, and pencil on
paperboard
16 × 18 inches
Stamped lower right:
*P. S. D. W. / Guernsey
Moore Collection / Gift of
Mrs. Moore*

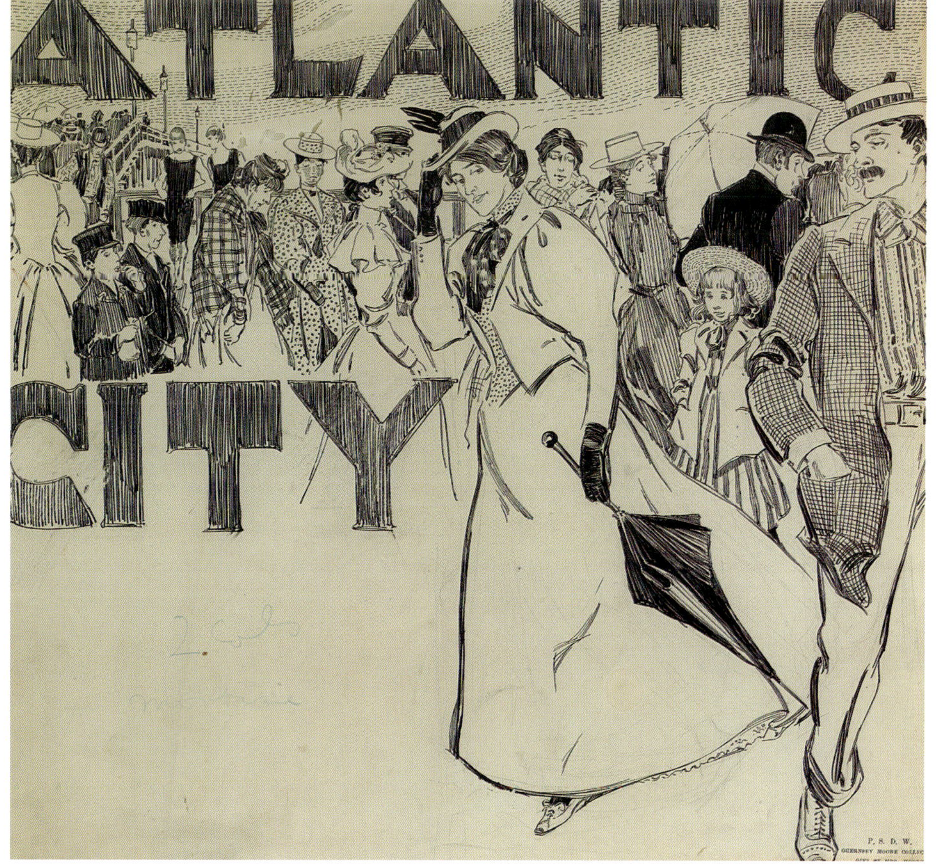

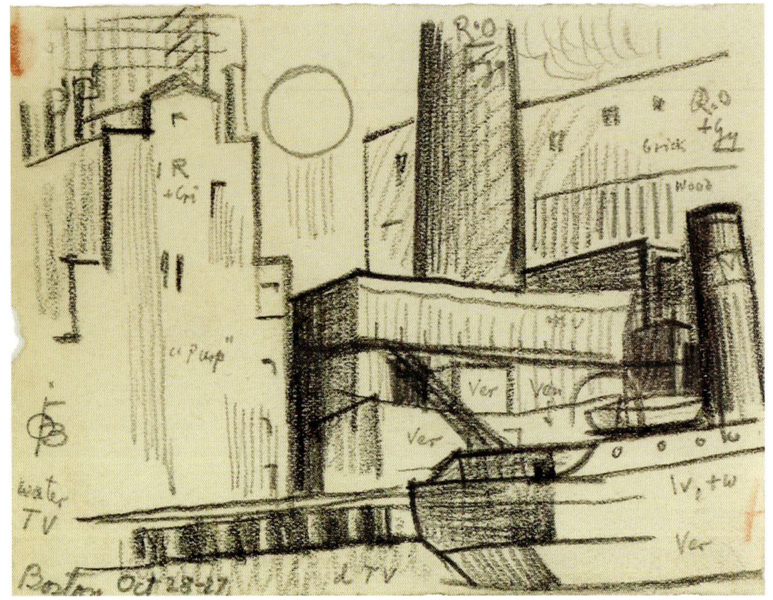

63.

Oscar Bluemner
(1867–1938)
Boston, 1927
Graphite on paper
3¾ × 5 inches
Signed with the artist's
monogrammed initials,
dated, and inscribed lower
left: *OFB / Boston Oct 28-27.*

64.

Oscar Bluemner
(1867–1938)
Stanhope (New Jersey), 1915
Graphite on paper
4½ × 5¾ inches
Signed with the artist's
monogrammed initials,
dated, and inscribed
lower left: *OFB / Stanhope
dy 13-15 rain.5.2P*

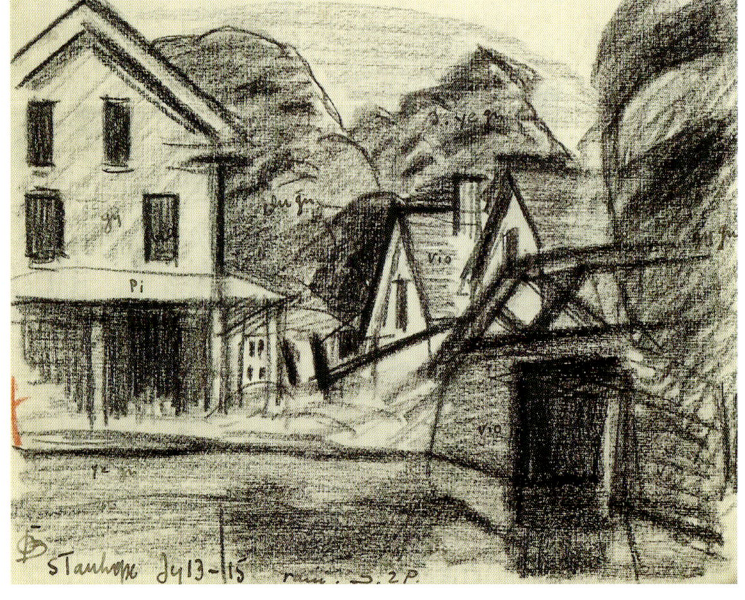

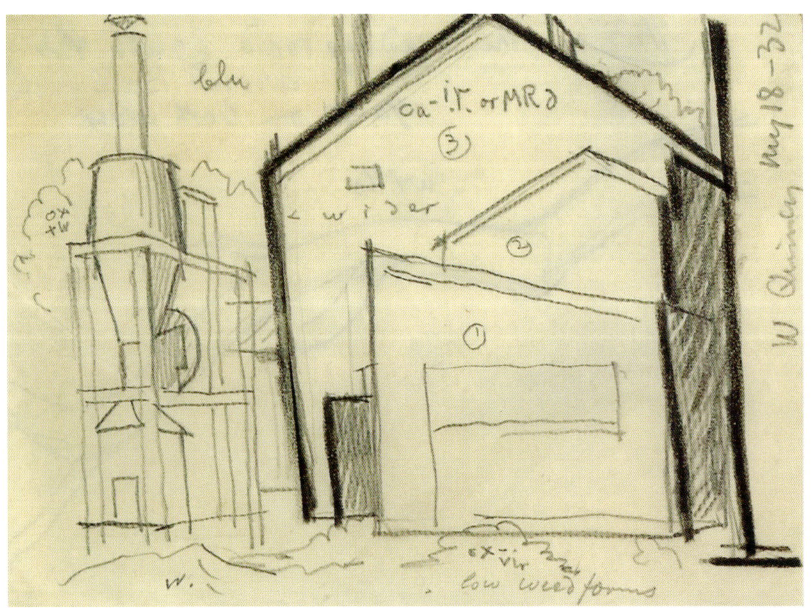

65.

Oscar Bluemner
(1867–1938)
West Quincy
(Massachusetts), 1932
Graphite on paper
4 × 5½ inches
Dated and inscribed in
right margin: *W Quincy
May 18-32*; Sketch and
inscribed on verso: *#3 The
Winding Road South of & /
around Ball* [illeg.] */ yards
on both sides.*

66.

Oscar Bluemner

(1867–1938)

Blackwells Hills, Raritan Canal (New Jersey), 1911
Colored crayon on paper
7½ × 5½ inches
Signed with the artist's monogrammed initials, dated, and inscribed lower right: *OFB / Blackwells Hills / 5.5-11-4.30 P.M. / ME. Raritan / Canal.*

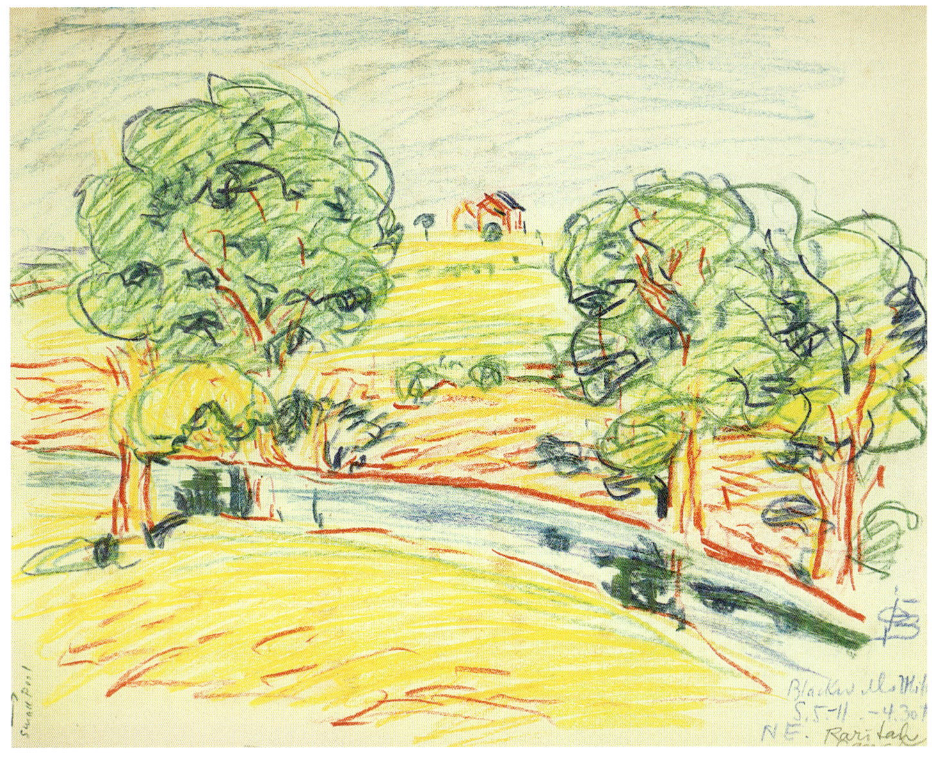

67.

Oscar Bluemner

(1867–1938)

Glendale (New Jersey), 1911
Colored crayon on paper
5 × 7½ inches
Signed with the artist's monogrammed initials, dated, and inscribed lower left: *OFB / A30-11 W5P Glendale.*; Inscribed on verso: *#18 6 85-LH*

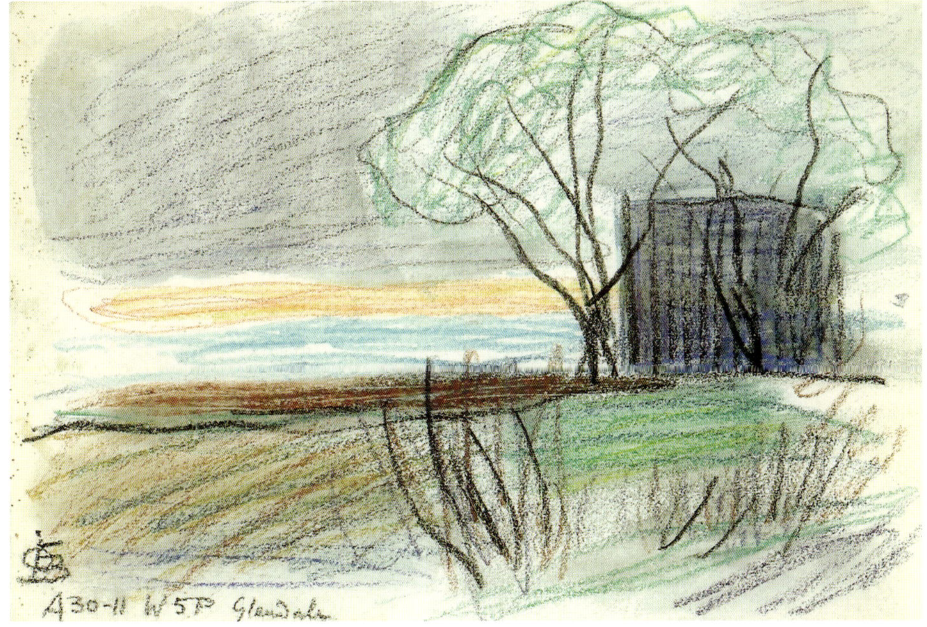

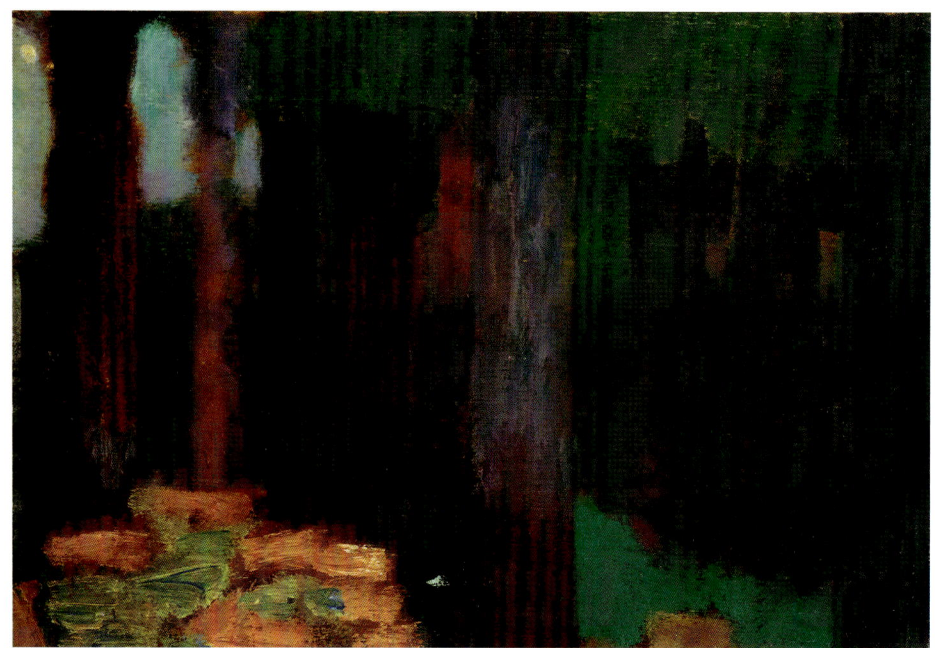

68.
George F. Of (1876–1954)
Untitled, ca. 1910
Oil on panel
5¼ × 7⅞ inches
Oil sketch on verso

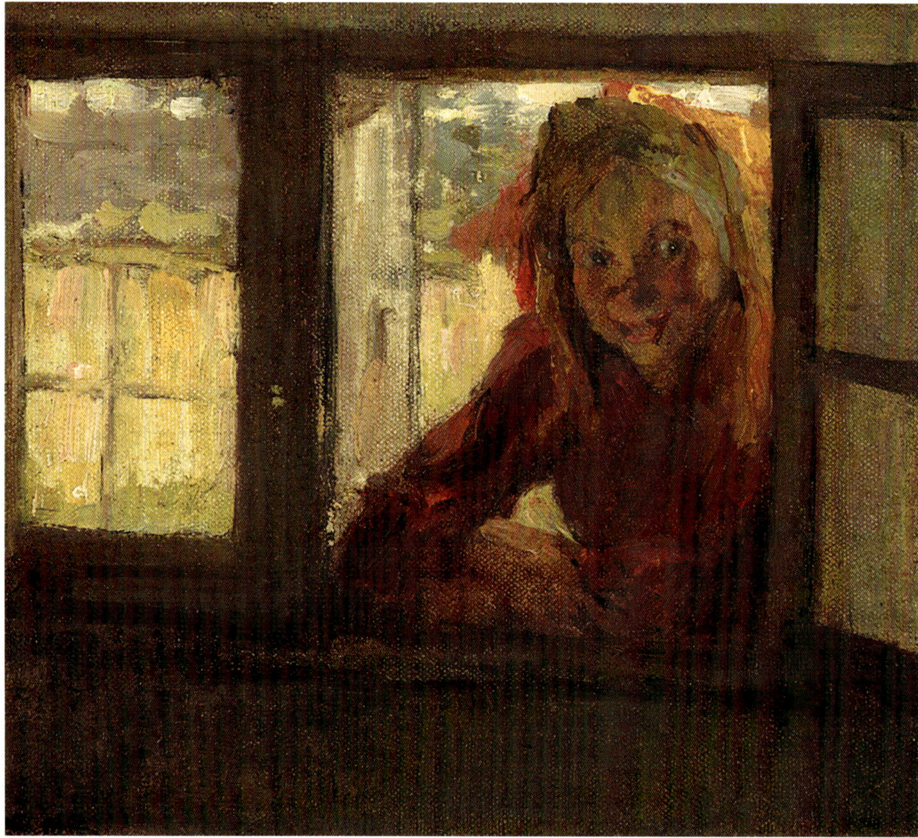

69.
Joseph Raphael
(1869–1950)
A Playful Moment,
ca. 1920–25
Oil on canvas
8½ × 9½ inches

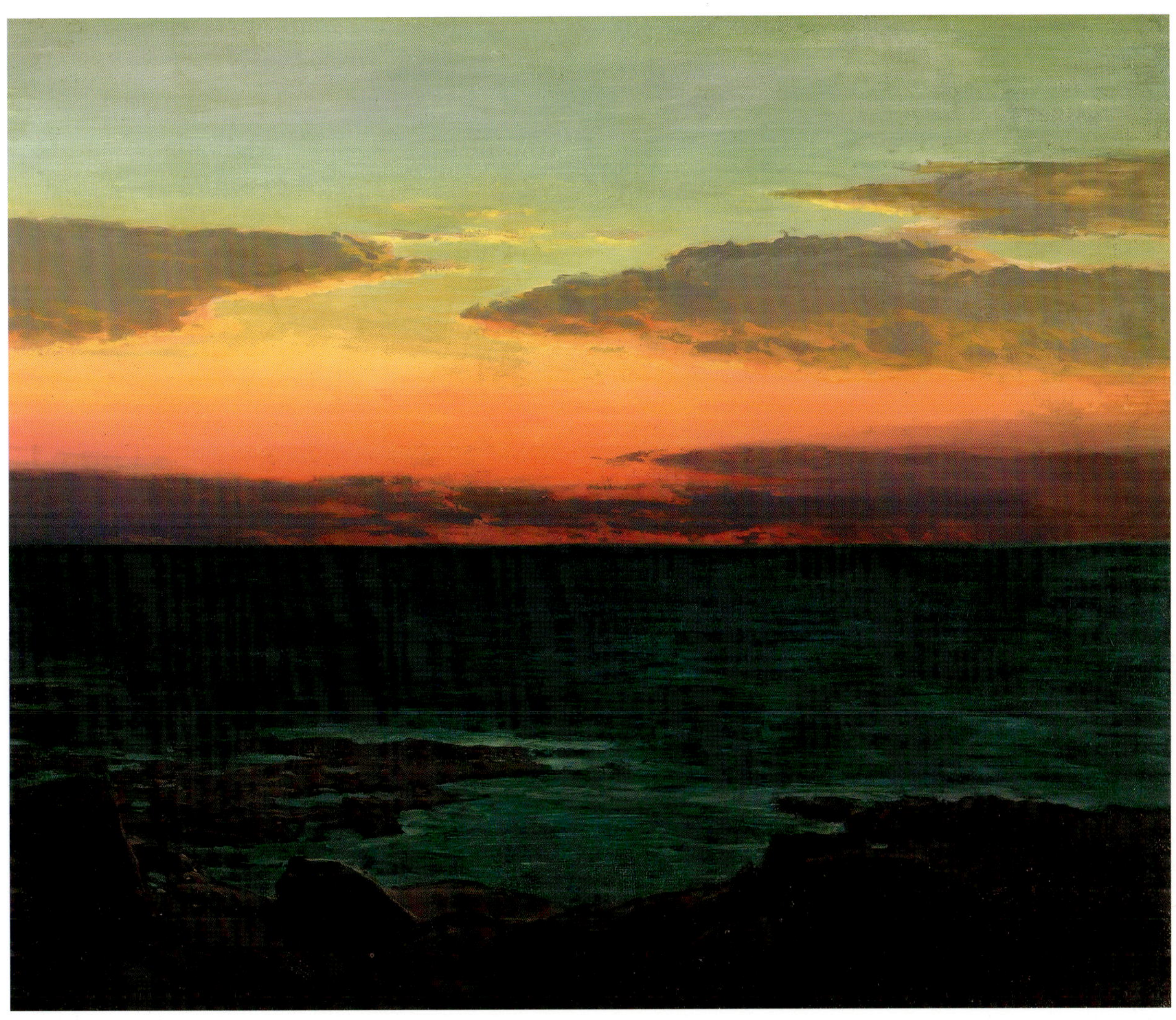

70.
Frederick Judd Waugh (1861–1940)
Crimson Dawn, ca. 1930
Oil on board, 23 × 28 inches
Signed lower right: *Waugh*
Inscribed on verso: *Crimson Dawn*

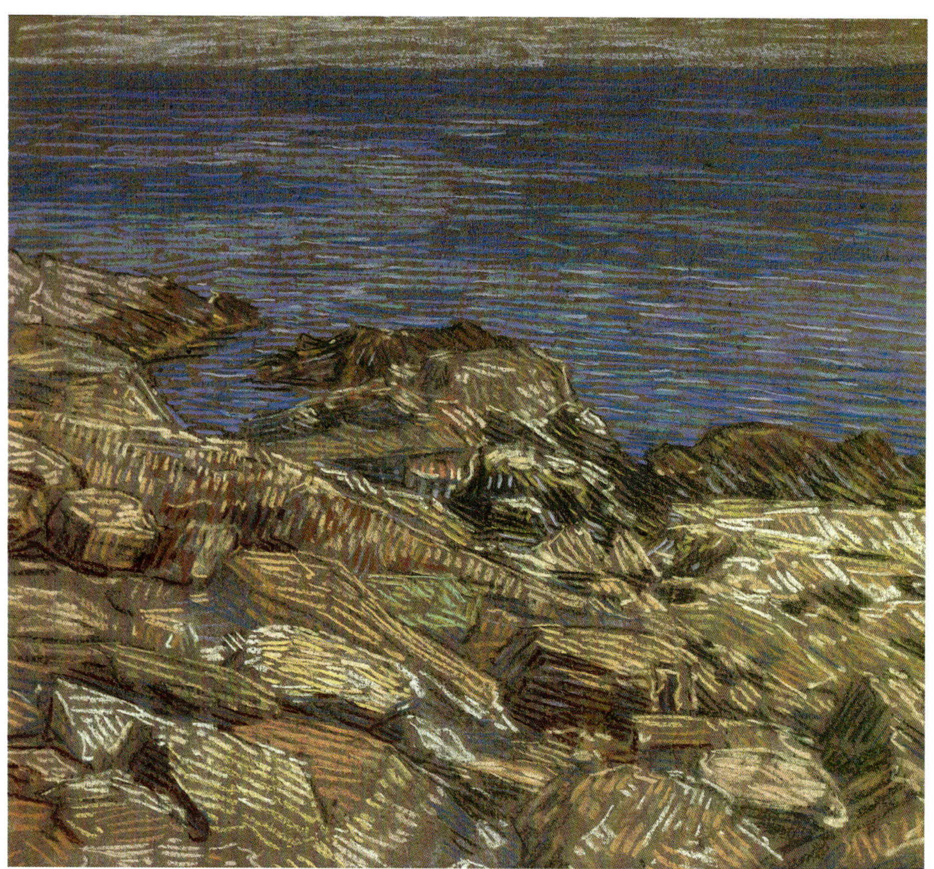

71.
Charles Salis Kaelin
(1858–1929)
Rocky Coast (Cape Ann,
Massachusetts),
ca. 1910s–20s
Pastel on paper
15¾ × 17½ inches
Signed lower left:
C. S. Kaelin

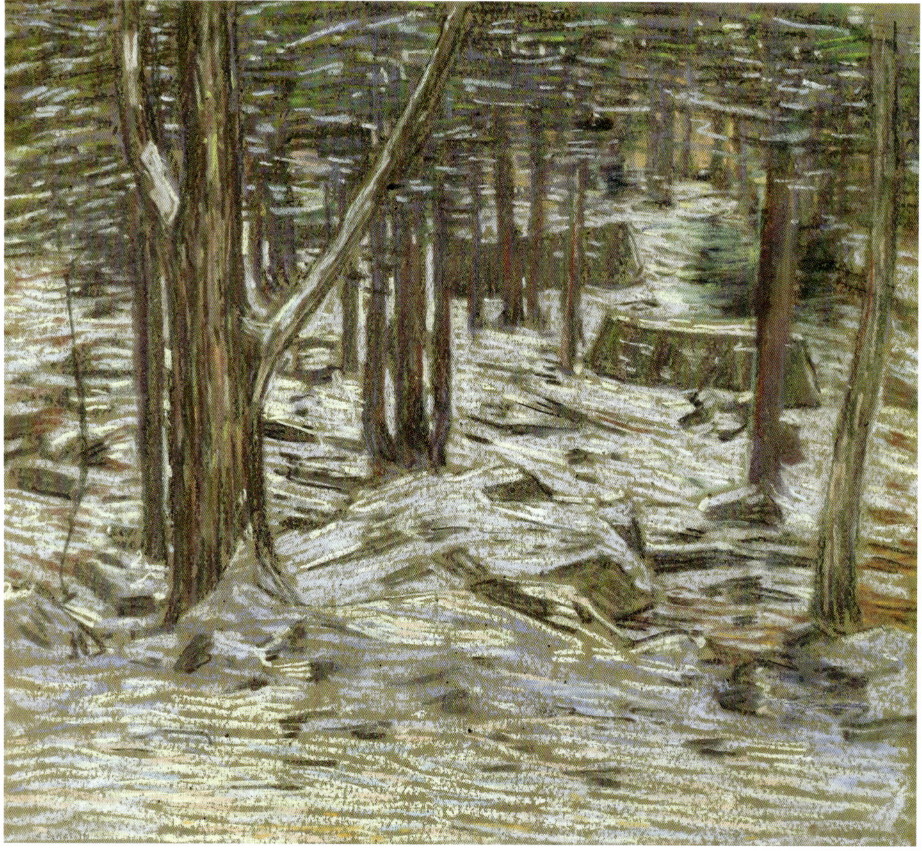

72.
Charles Salis Kaelin
(1858–1929)
Snow in the Woods
(Rockport, Massachusetts),
ca. 1920
Pastel on paper
16 × 17¾ inches
Signed lower left:
C. S. Kaelin.

73.
Sándor Bernath
(1892–1985)
Dockside, 1935
Watercolor on paper
mounted on board
18 × 16¼ inches
Signed and dated lower
left: *Sandor / Bernath 35.*

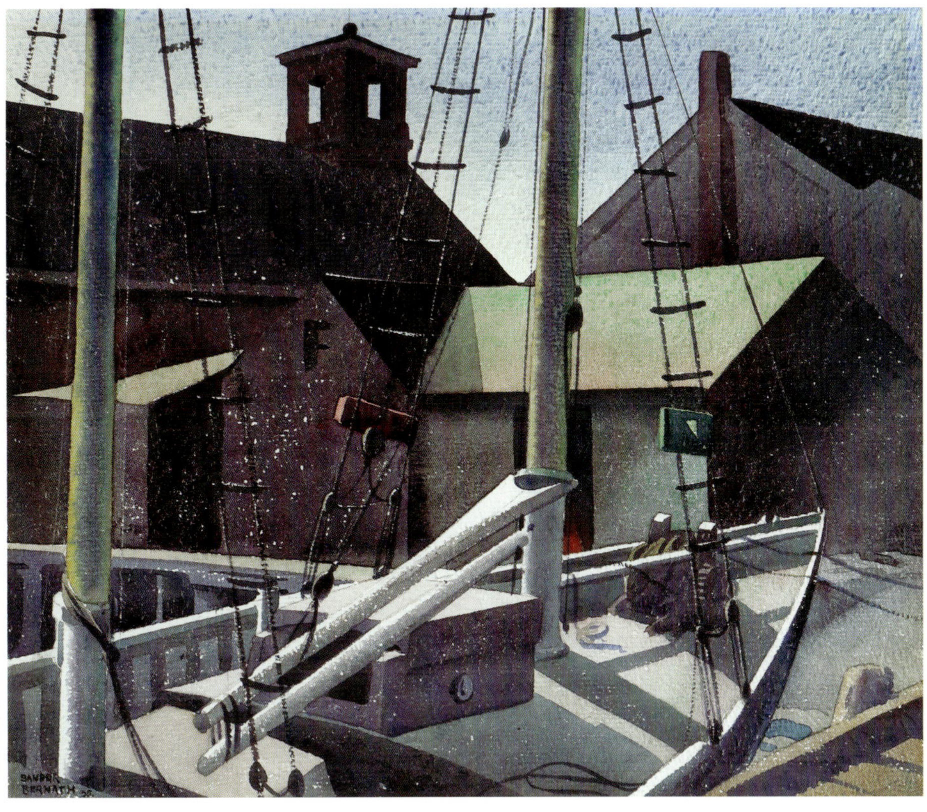

74.
Carlton M. Soule
(20th century)
Village Street
Oil on canvas
19 × 25 inches
Signed lower right: *Soule*

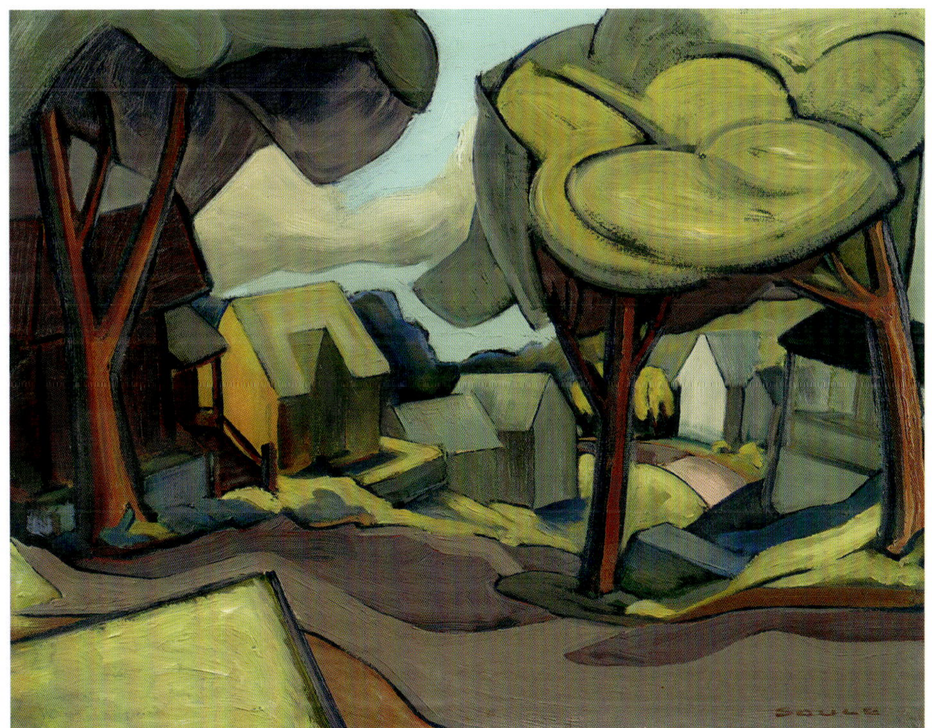

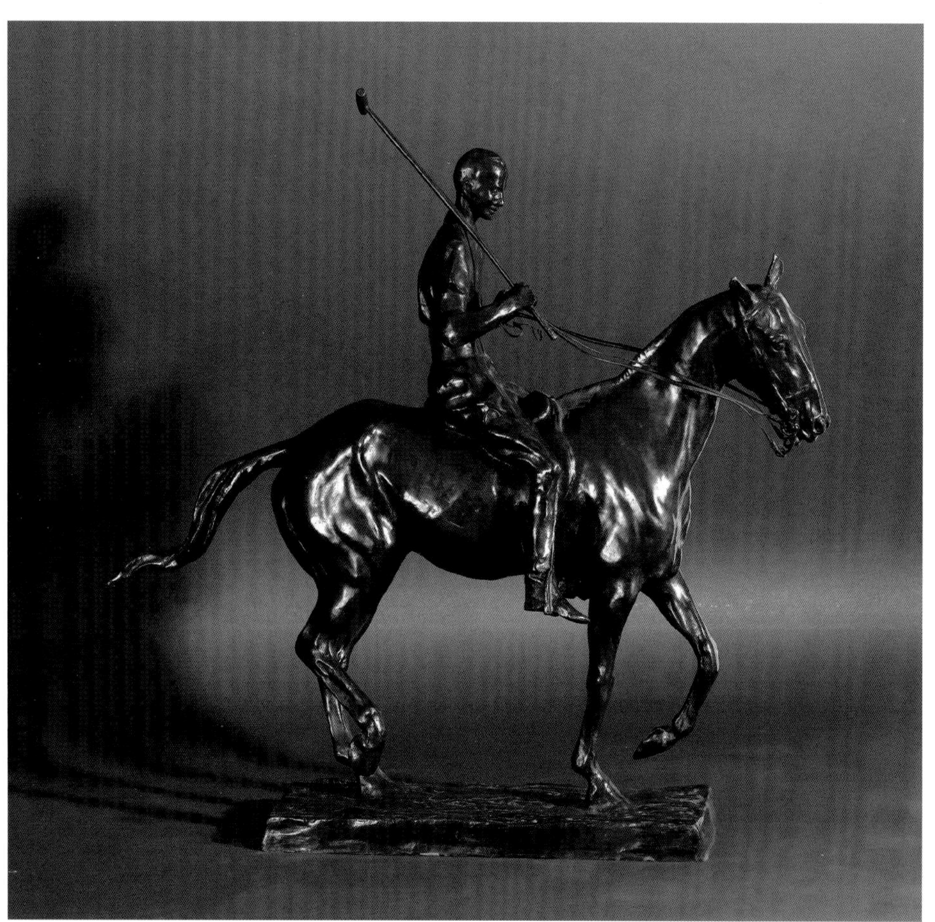

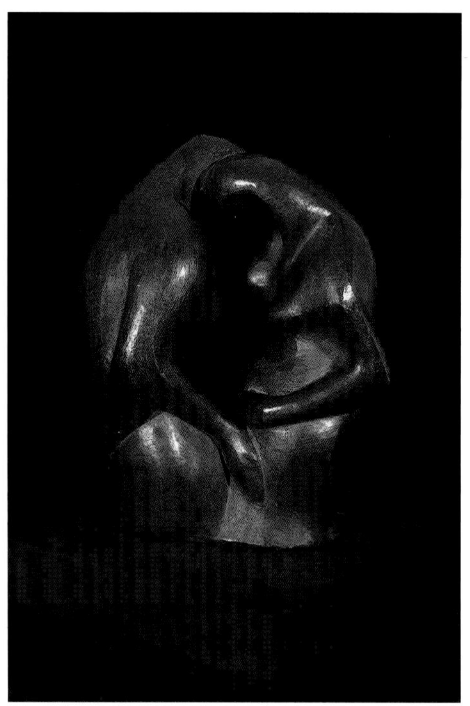

76.
Hugo Robus (1885–1964)
Two Women, ca. 1920s–30s
Painted plaster
Height: 8¾ inches
Signed on base: *Hugo Robus*

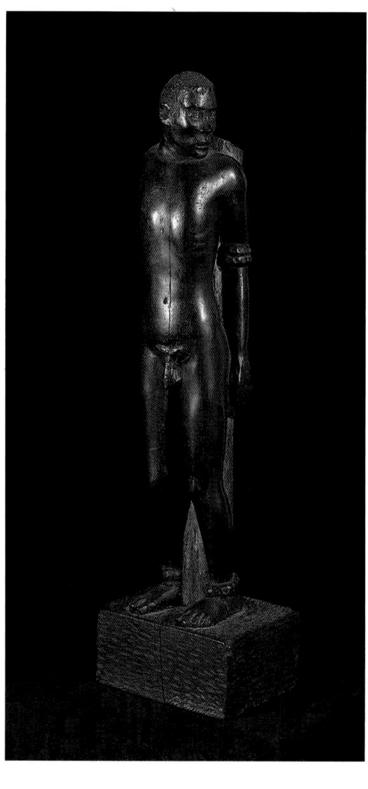

77.
Nathaniel Choate
(1899–1965)
Man in Bondage, ca. 1935
Carved ebonized wood
Height: 16 inches
Signed lower right on base:
N. Choate

78.
Eric Sloane (1905–1985)
*Night and Day at 8,000
Feet, Republic Lancers,*
ca. 1940
Oil on panel
30 × 25 inches
Signed lower right:
Eric Sloane

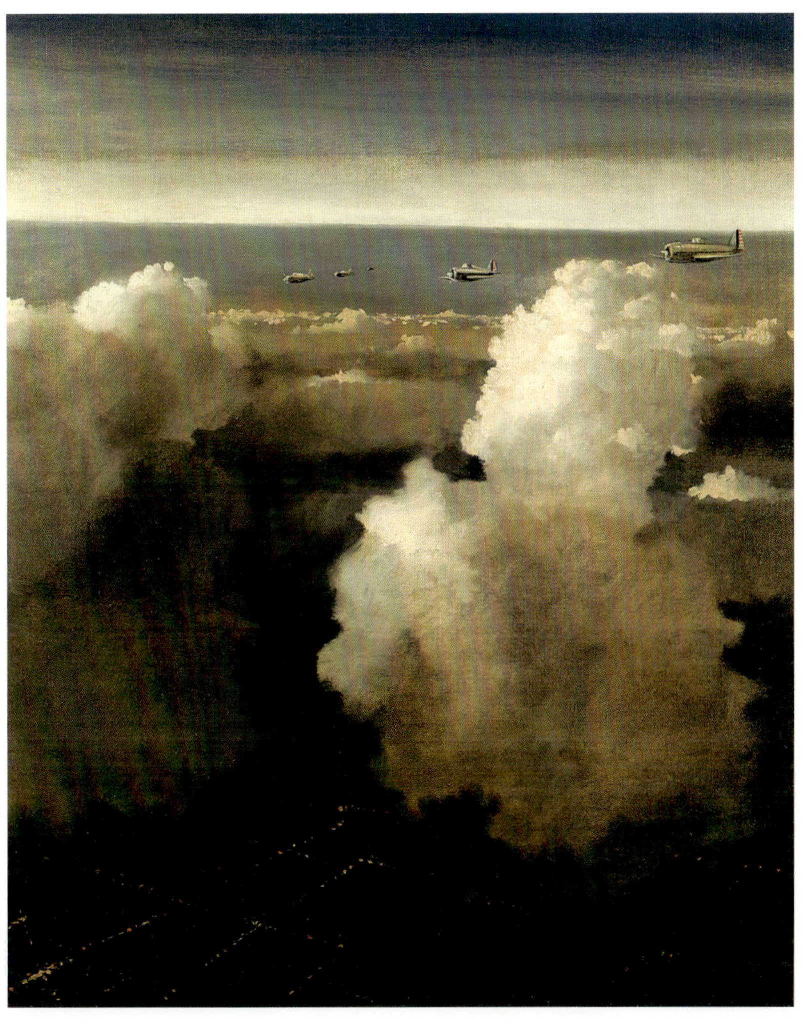

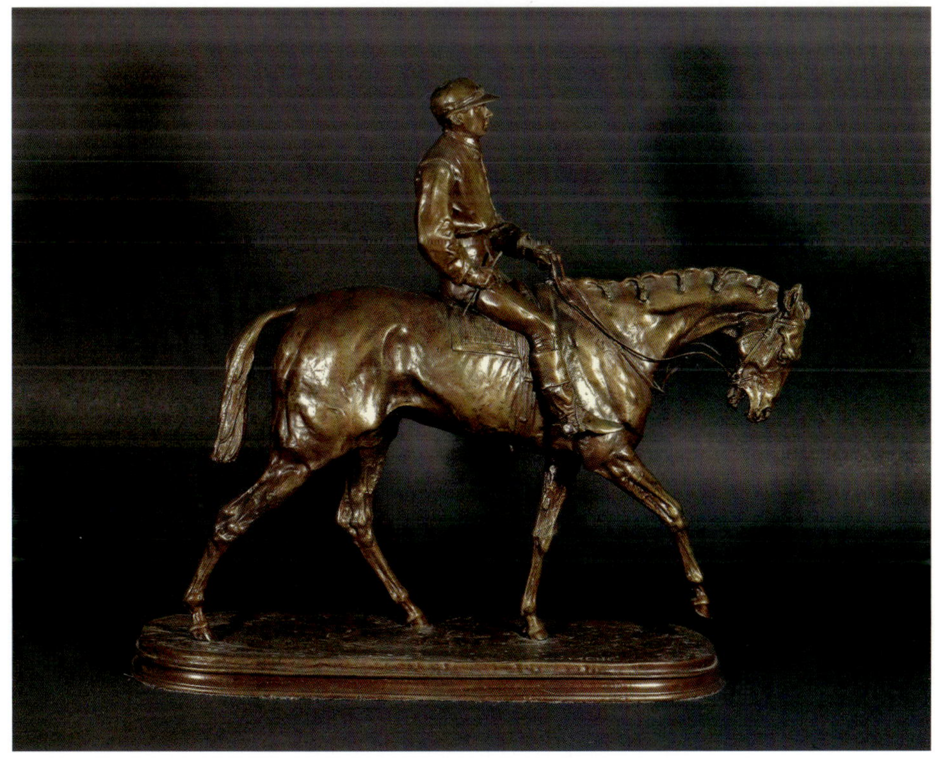

79.
**Attributed to
Pierre Jules Mène**
(French, 1810–1879)
Race Horse with Jockey Up,
ca. 1860s–70s
Bronze
Height: 17½ inches
Inscribed on base:
P. J. Mene

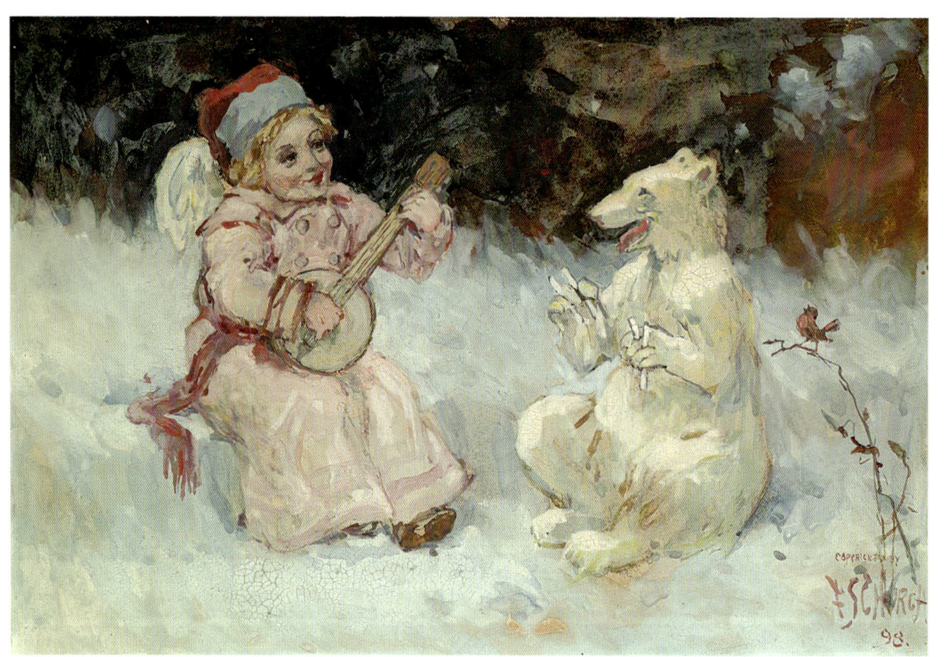

80.
Frederick Stuart Church
(1842–1924)
A Trio (Cherub, Polar Bear, and Bird), 1898
Gouache and watercolor on board
7¾ × 11¼ inches
Signed, dated, and inscribed lower right: *copyrighted by / F S Church / 98.*
Inscribed on verso: *A Trio*

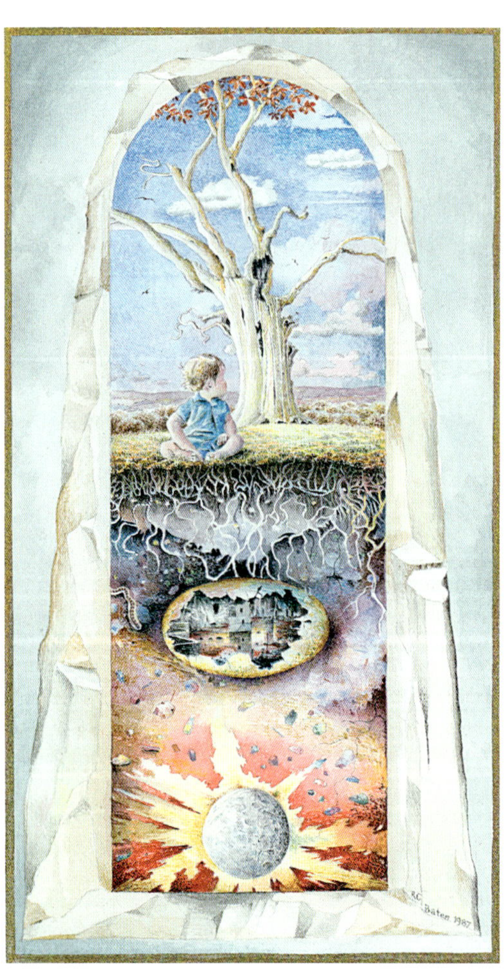

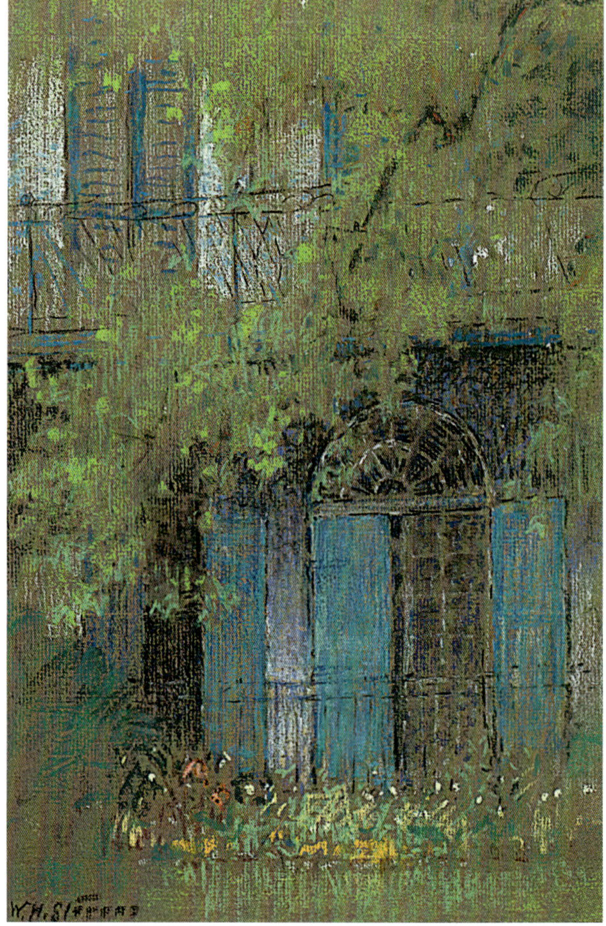

81.
Robert C. Bates (British, b. 1943)
On Earth, 1987
Watercolor on paper, 7 × 4 inches
Signed and dated lower right: *R. C. Bates. 1987.*

82.
Will Henry Stevens (1881–1949)
French Quarter Façade (New Orleans), ca. 1920s
Pastel on paper, 11½ × 7½ inches
Signed lower left: *W. H. Stevens*

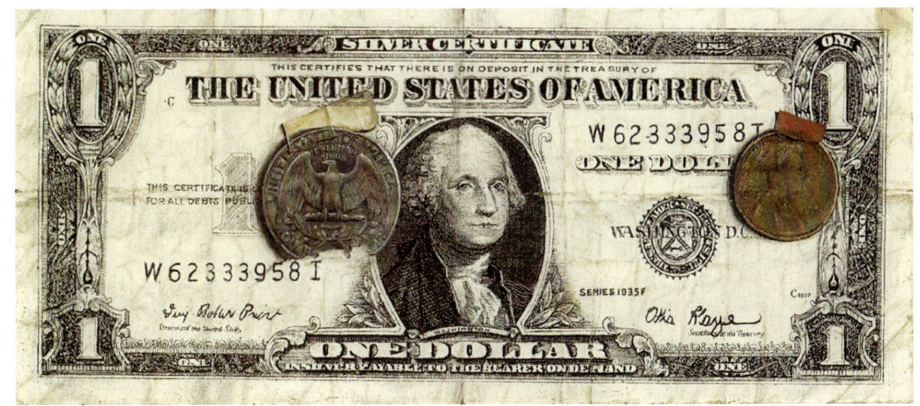

83.
Otis Kaye (1885–1974)
One Dollar Note with a Quarter and a Penny,
after 1935
Oil, watercolor, and ink on paper
2¾ × 6¹⁄₁₆ inches
Signed lower right:
Otis Kaye

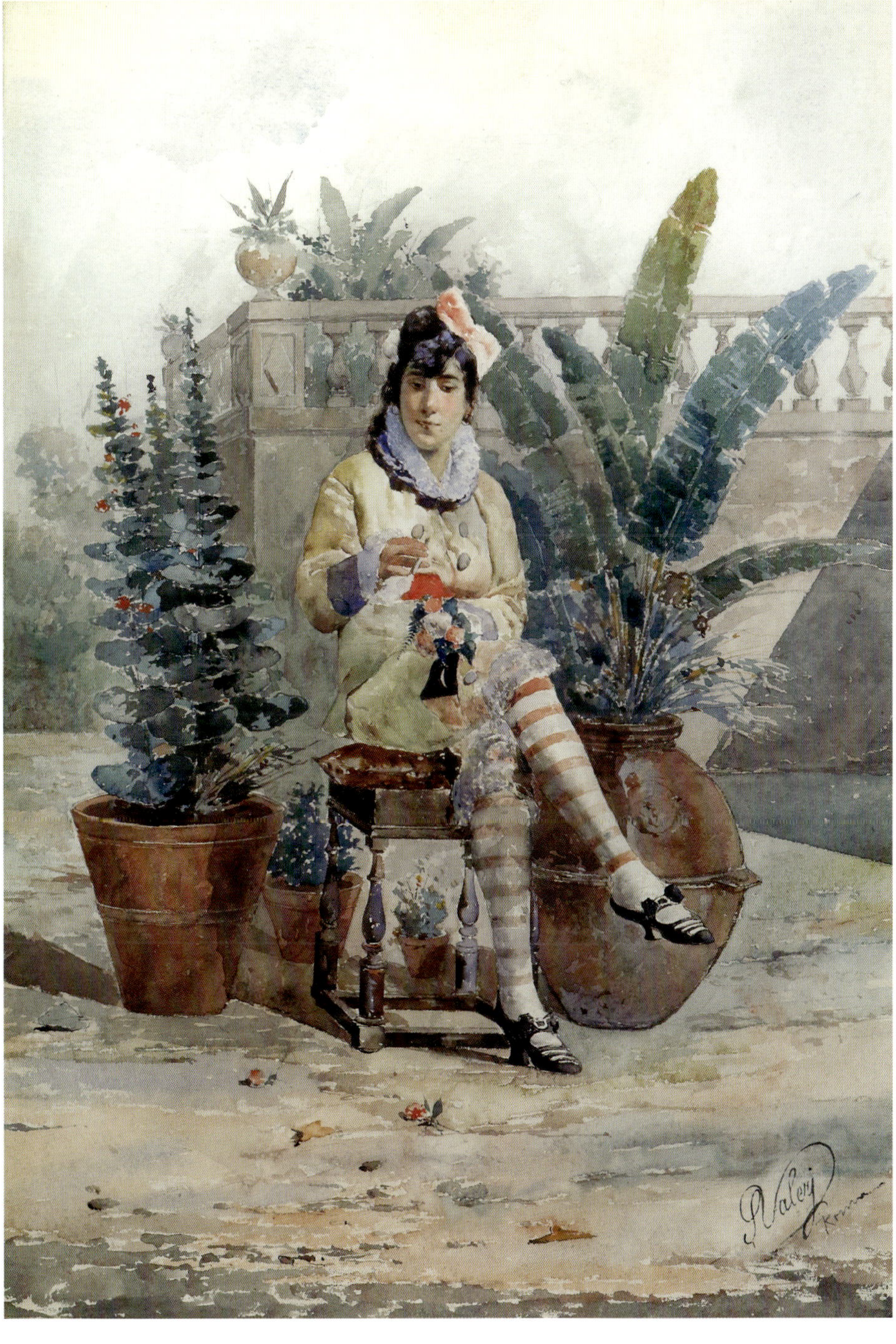

84.
P. Valeri (19th century)
A Reflective Moment
Watercolor over pencil on paper
20⅜ × 14⅛ inches
Signed lower right: *P. Valeri*

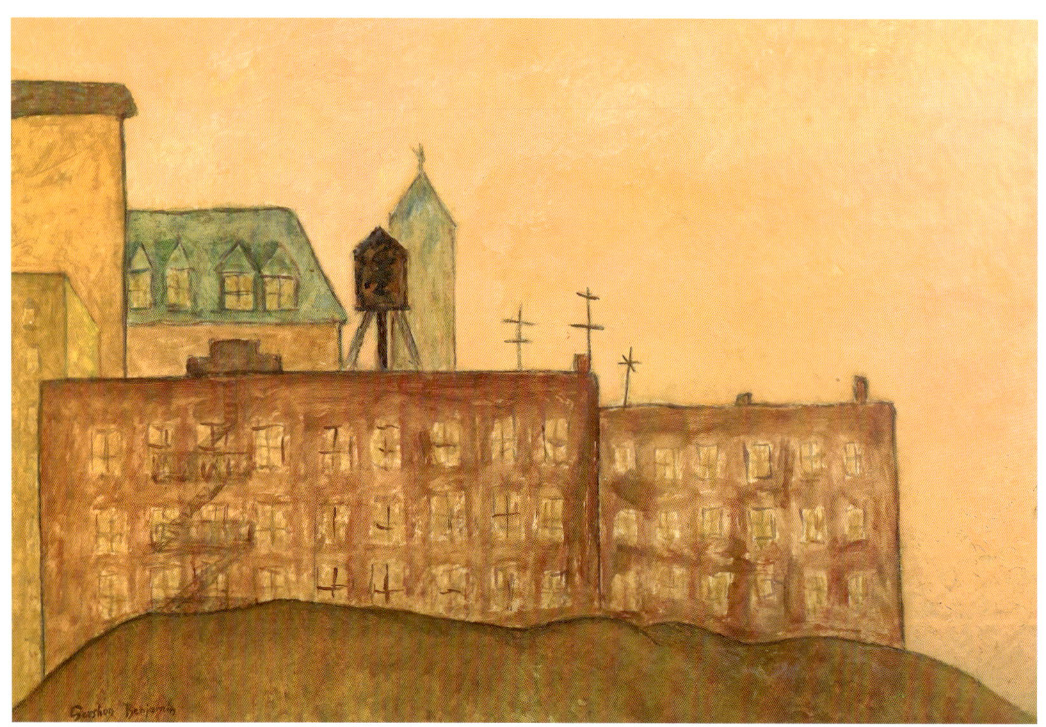

85.
Gershon Benjamin (1899–1985)
City Scope (New York), 1975
Acrylic on canvas, 24 × 36 inches
Signed lower left: *Gershon Benjamin*; Signed, dated, and inscribed
on verso: *#288 City Scope by Gershon Benjamin 24 x 36 1975*

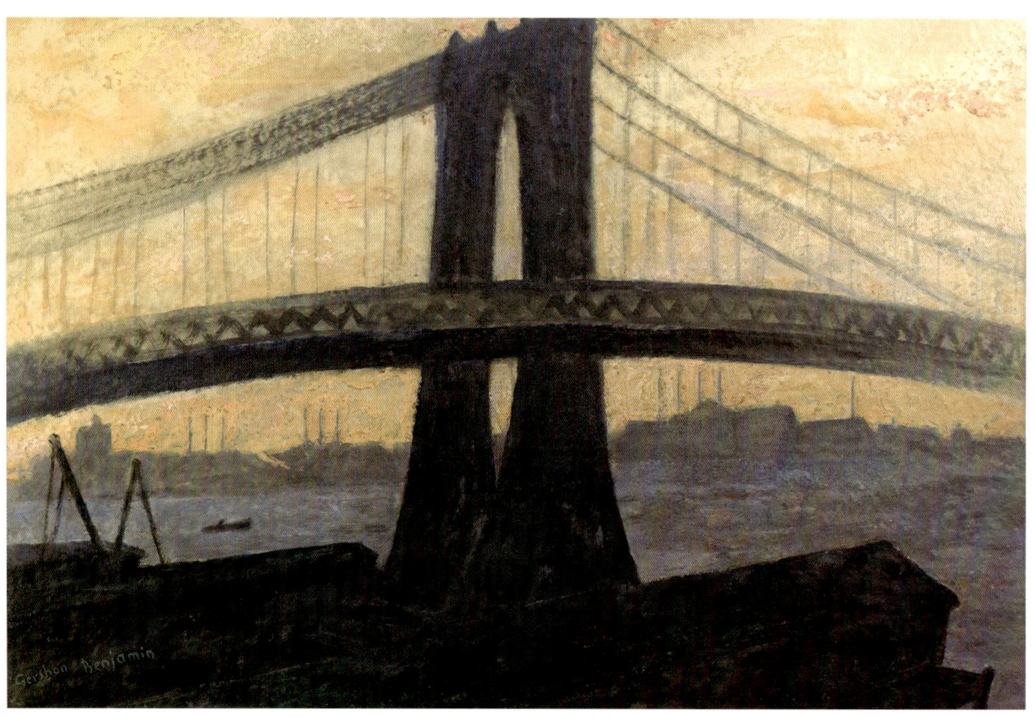

86.
Gershon Benjamin (1899–1985)
Brooklyn Bridge at Sunrise (New York), 1968
Oil on paper mounted on board, 24 × 36 inches
Signed lower left: *Gershon Benjamin*; Signed, dated, and
inscribed on verso: *#136 Title / Brooklyn Bridge / at /
Sunrise / by Gershon Benjamin 1968*

87.
Louis Aston Knight
(1873–1948)
*The George Washington
Bridge seen from the
Upper West Side* (New
York), ca. 1930s–40s
Oil on board
10¾ × 17 inches
Signed and inscribed
lower right: *Aston Knight
New York*

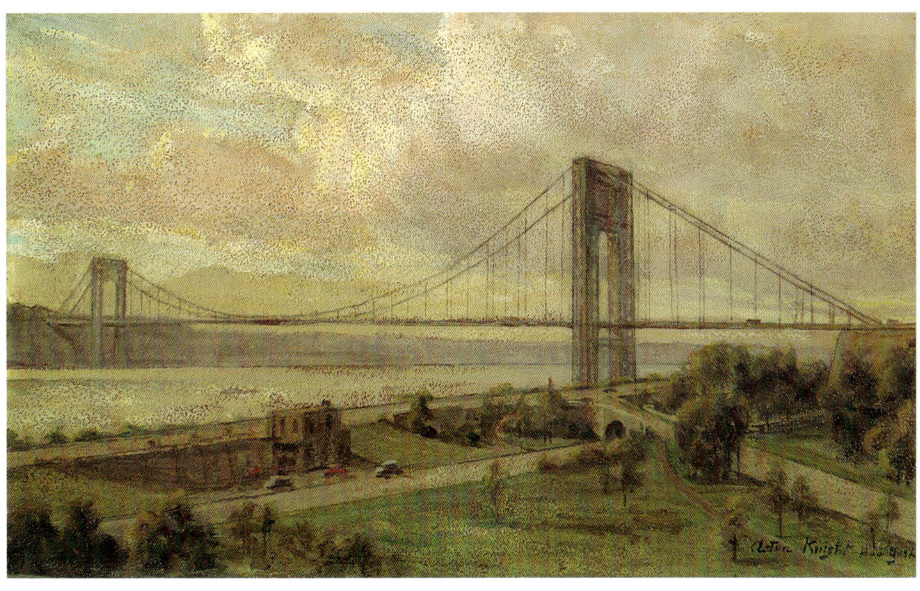

88.
Stuyvesant Van Veen
(1910–1988)
*Late Afternoon, Staten
Island* (New York), ca. 1950s
Gouache on paper
mounted on board
17¼ × 13¼ inches
Signed lower right:
Stuyvesant Van Veen / [illeg.]

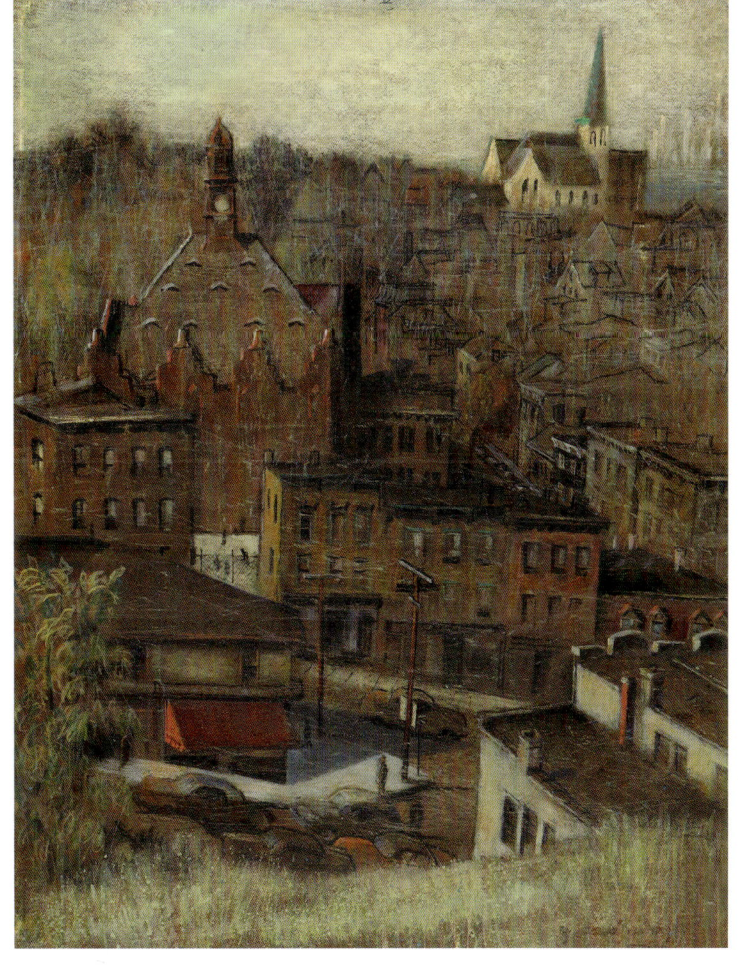

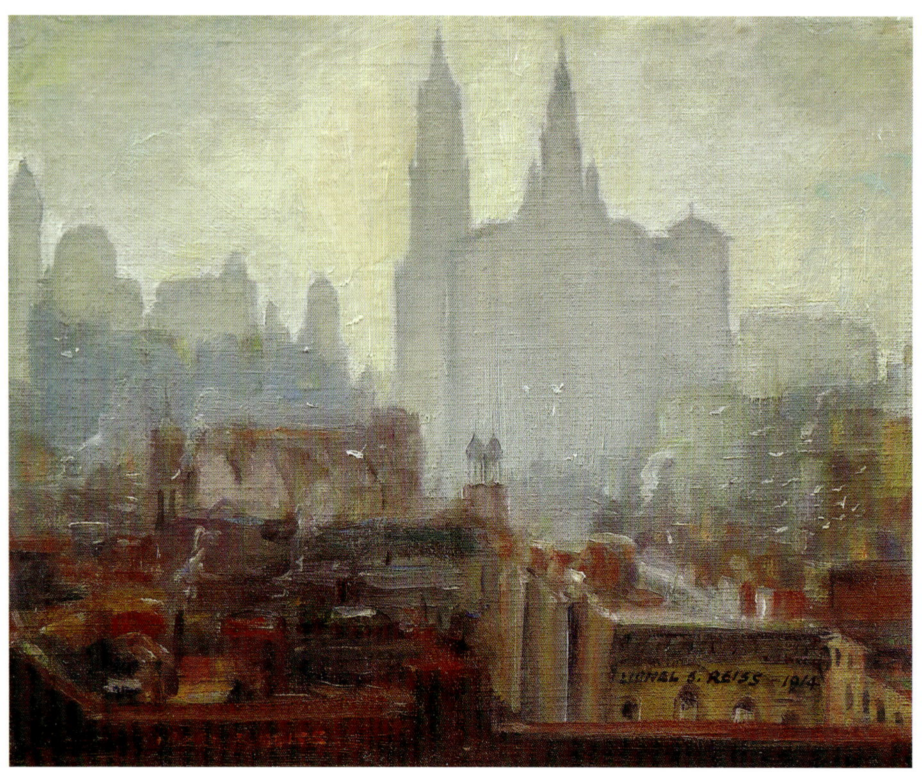

89.
Lionel S. Reiss (1894–1988)
Municipal and Woolworth Buildings, Lower Manhattan, 1914
Oil on board
8 × 10 inches
Signed and dated lower right: *Lionel S. Reiss—1914*

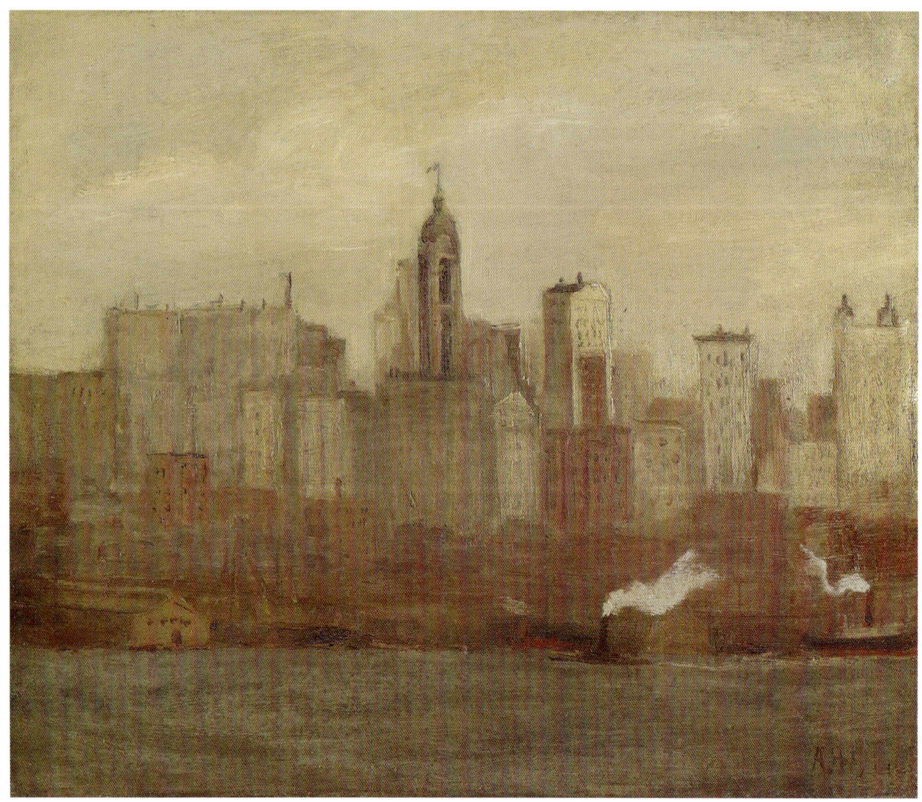

90.
Aaron Harry Gorson
(1872–1933)
New York City Skyline, 1909
Oil on canvas
14⅛ × 17 inches
Signed and dated lower right: *A. H. G. / 09*

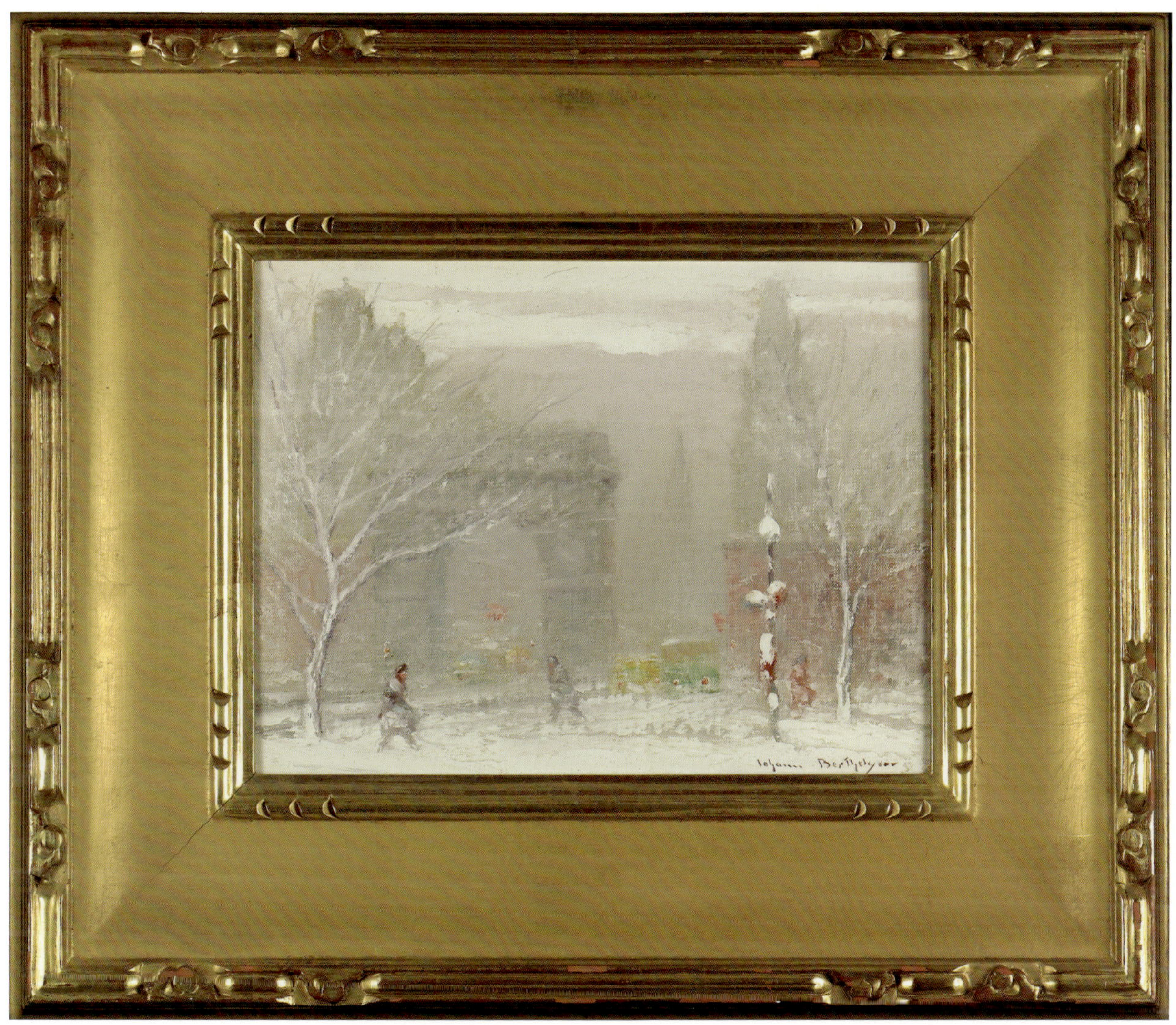

91.
Johann Berthelsen (1883–1972)
Washington Square Arch in Winter (New York), ca. 1930s–40s
Oil on canvasboard, 9 × 12 inches
Signed lower right: *Johann Berthelsen*

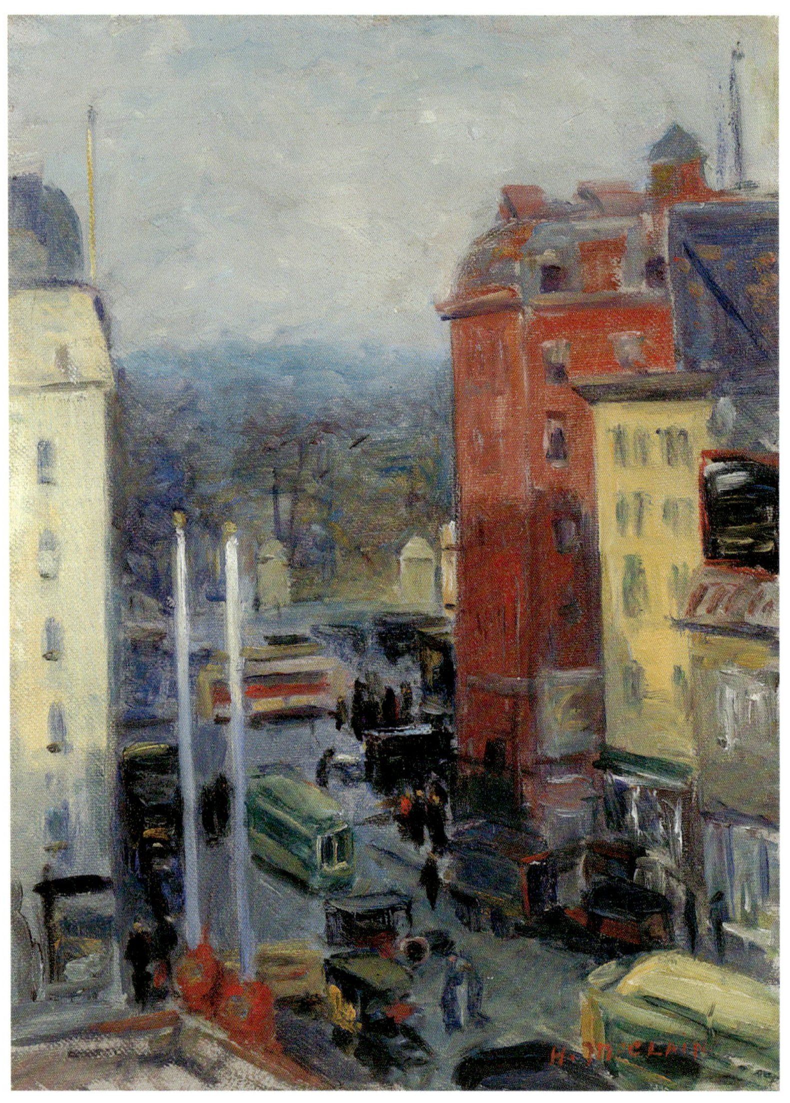

92.
Helen Charlton McClain
(b. 1887–active 1940)
*New York Street
Scene*, ca. 1920
Oil on canvas
16¼ × 12 inches
Signed lower right:
H. McClain

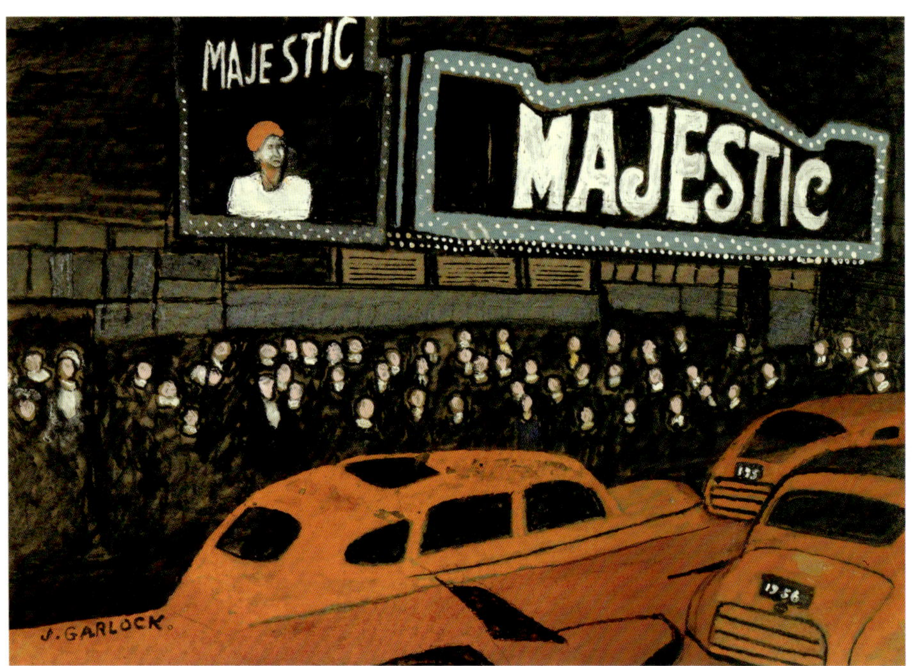

93.
Joseph Garlock
(1884–1980)
*Majestic Theater, New York
City*, 1956
Gouache on board
10 × 14½ inches
Signed lower left: *J. Garlock.*
Dated lower right: *1956*

94.
Peter Plamondon (b. 1939)
White Dishes, 1991
Oil on canvas
36 × 32 inches
Signed with the artist's
initials lower right: *P. P.*;
Signed and dated on verso:
Peter Plamondon 1991

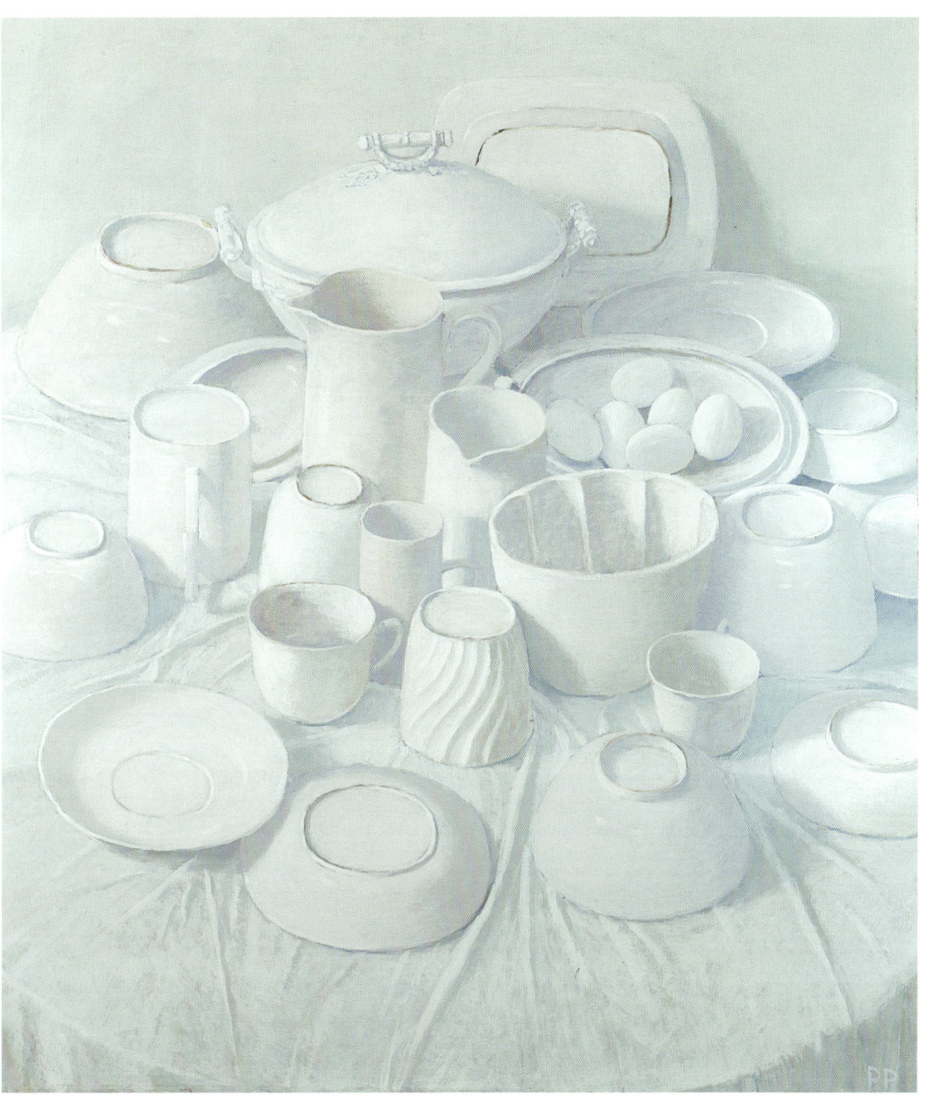

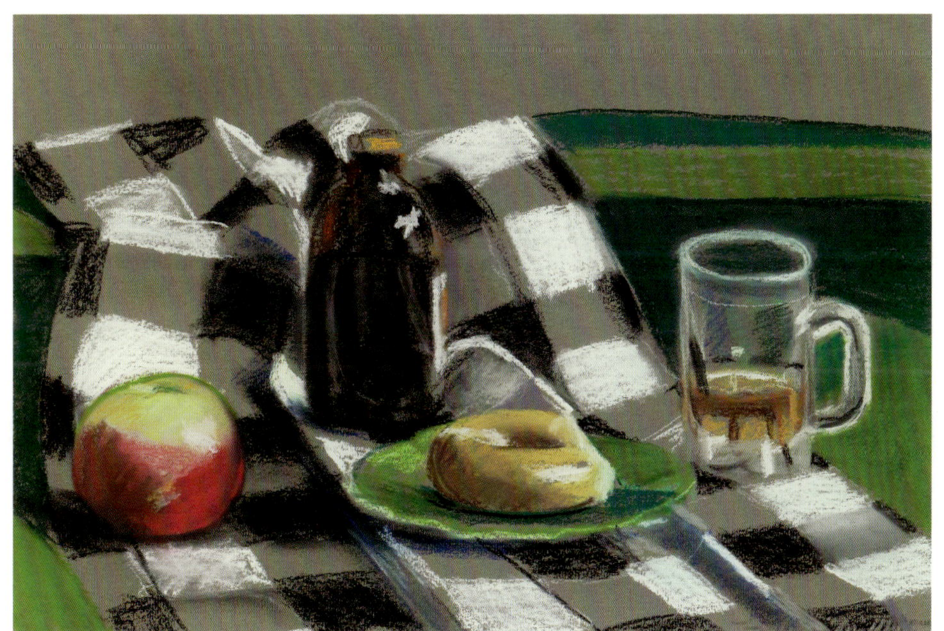

95.
Louisa Matthiasdottir
(1917–2000)
*Apples, Bread, and
Beer,* ca. 1940s
Pastel on paper
12¼ × 18¼ inches
Signed lower right: *Louisa
Matthiasdottir*; Estate
number stamped lower
right: *N. 129*

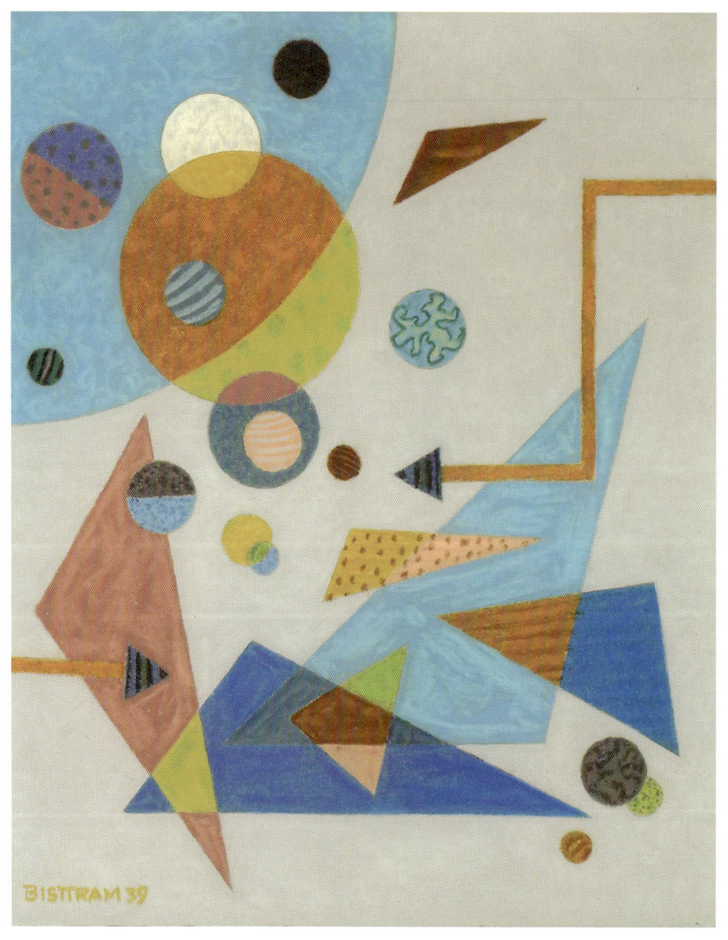

96.
Emil Bisttram (1895–1976)
Abstraction, 1939
Gouache and colored
pencil on paper
11 × 9 inches
Signed and dated lower
left: *Bisttram 39*

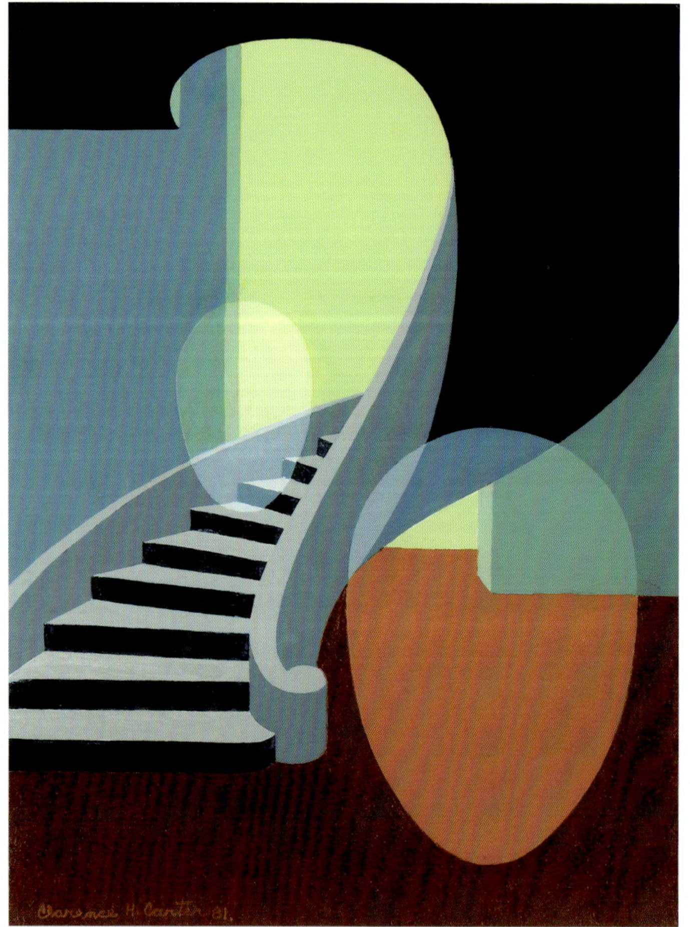

97.
Clarence Holbrook Carter
(1904–2000)
Study for Appearance, 1981
Acrylic on paper
10⅜ × 7⅞ inches
Signed and dated lower
left: *Clarence H. Carter 81.*

98.
Charles Green Shaw
(1892–1974)
Polygon Forty-Four, 1968
Oil on canvas
8 × 10 inches
Signed and dated on verso:
Charles Shaw / 1968

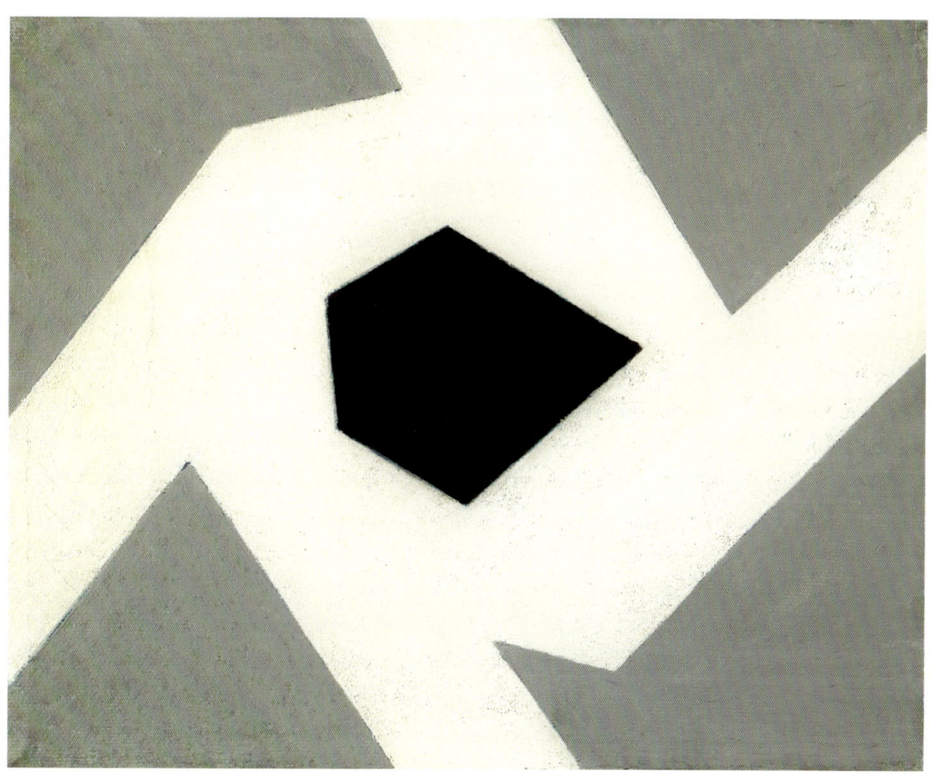

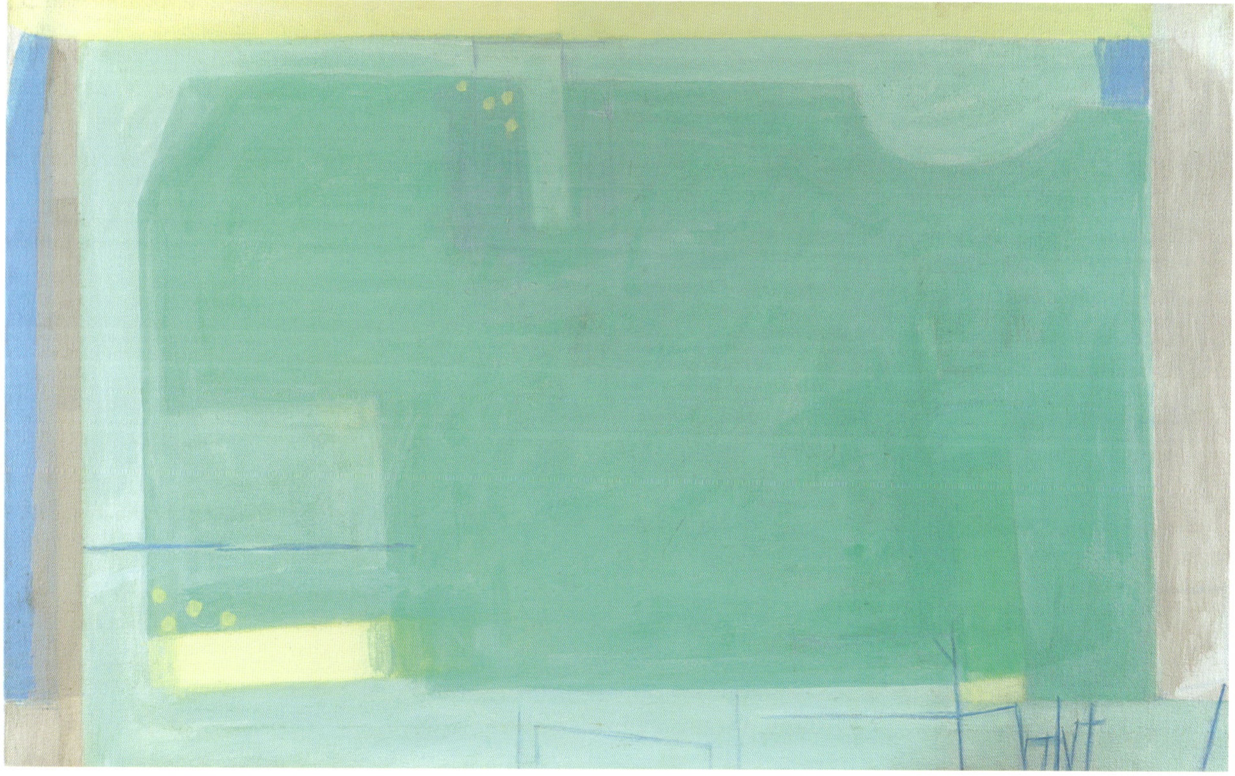

99.
Simeon Braguin (1907–1997)
Untitled, 1986
Watercolor on paper, 26 × 42 inches
Signed and dated on verso: *Simeon Braguin '86*

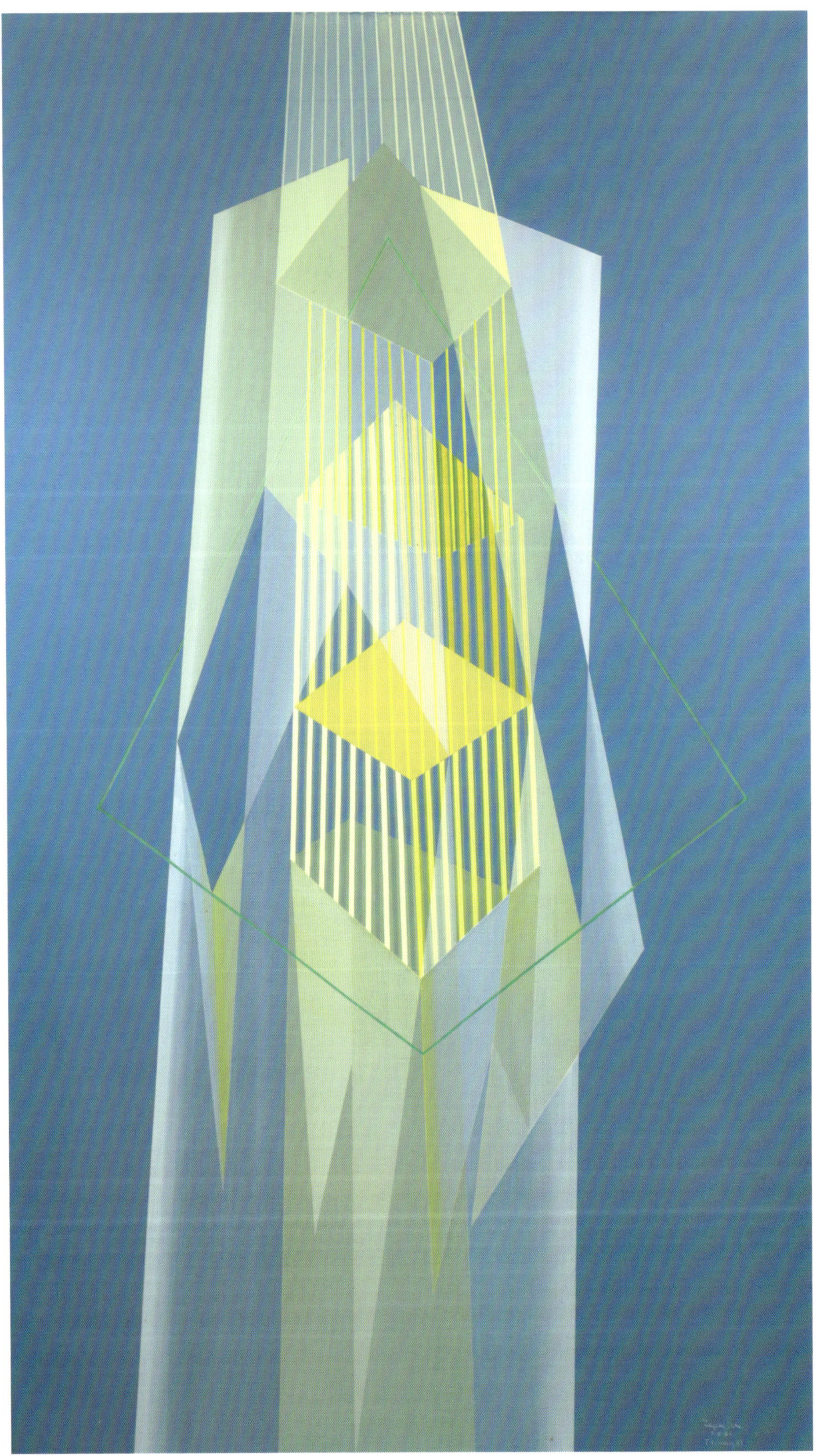

100.
Eugene Dana (1912–1987)
Celestial Cage, 1983
Acrylic on board
54 × 31 inches
Signed and dated lower
right: *Eugene Dana / 5-5-82
/ 7 February 83*; Estate label
on verso

101.
Eugene Dana (1912–1987)
Summertime, 1987
Acrylic on board
49½ × 49½ inches
Signed and dated lower
right: *Eugene Dana / 1980/4
87*; Estate label on verso

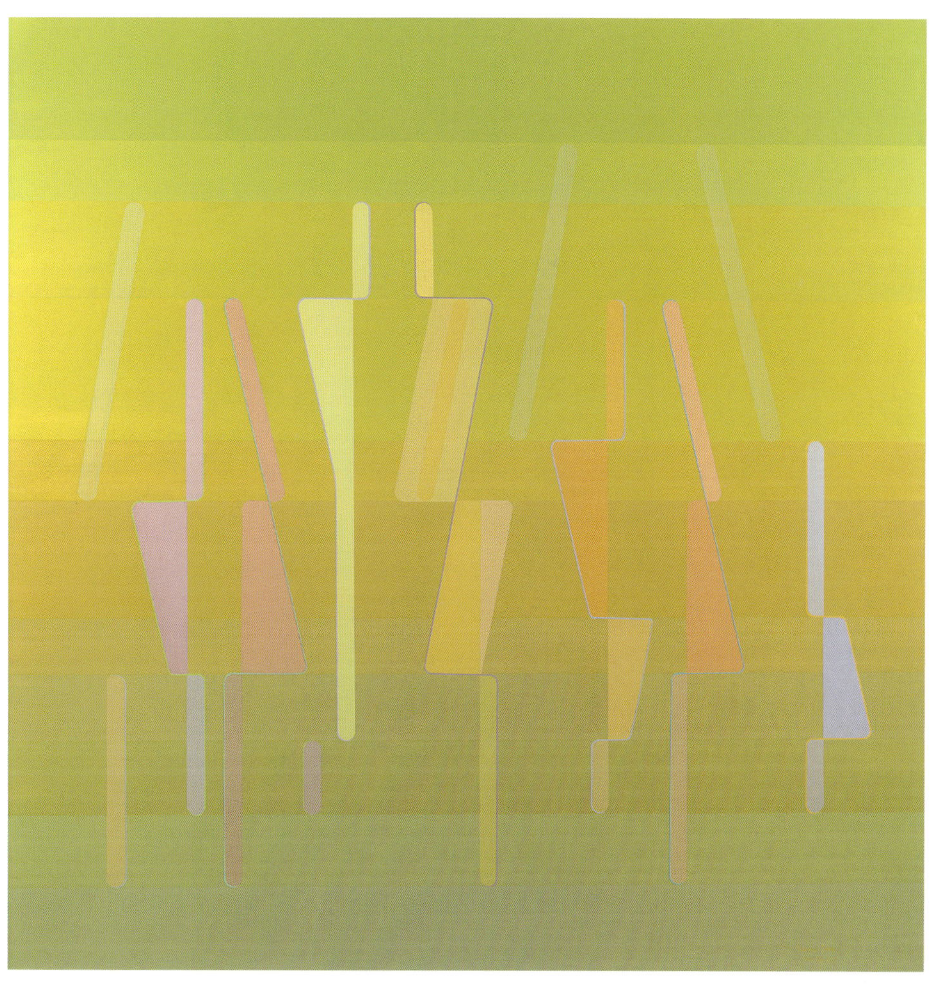

102.
Louis Schanker (1903–1981)
Abstract (Red), 1945
Gouache and watercolor
on paper
27 × 20 inches
Signed and dated lower
right: *Schanker—45*

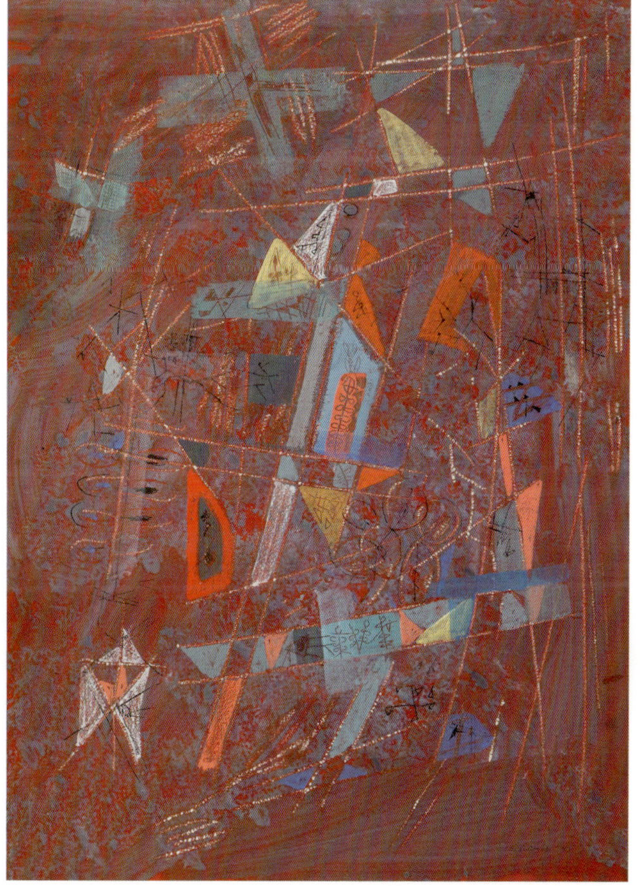

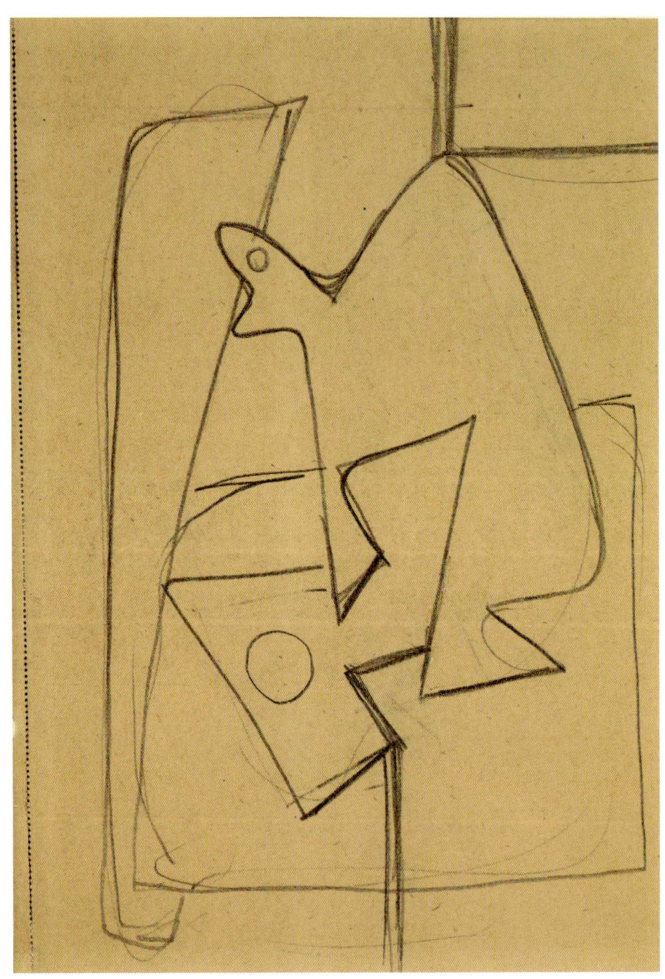

103.
Arshile Gorky (1904–1948)
Still Life Abstraction,
ca. 1935–36
Graphite on paper
11⅛ × 8 inches
Sketch on verso

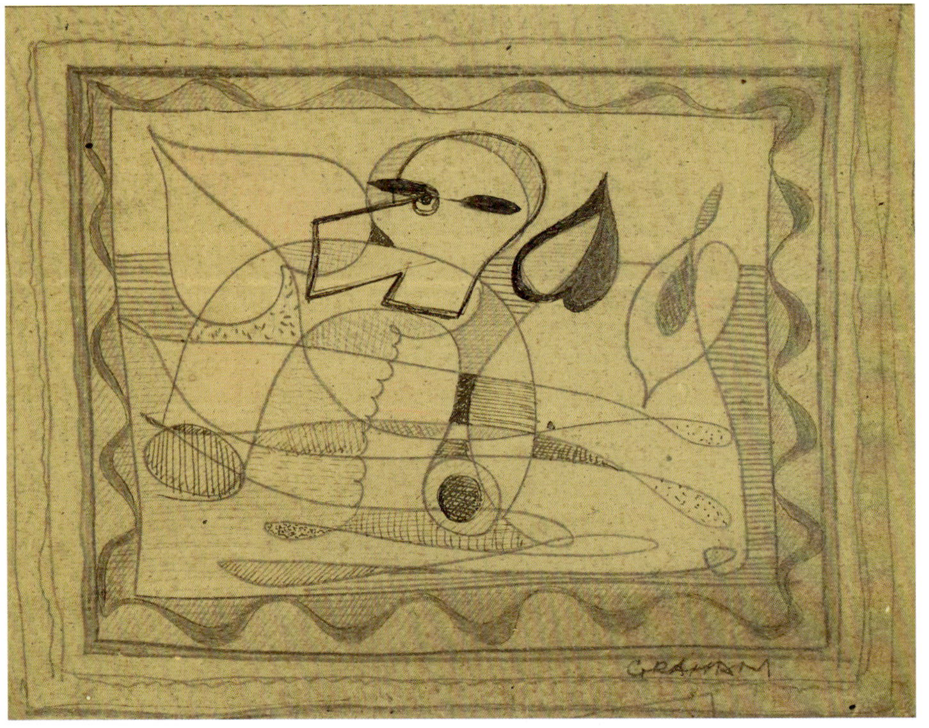

104.
John Graham (1886–1961)
Abstract, ca. 1930s
Pencil, ink, and crayon
on paper
9¼ × 11⅝ inches
Signed lower right:
Graham

105.
Stanley Bielecky
(1903–1985)
Untitled (Green), ca. 1940
Colored crayon on paper
8¾ × 5¾ inches
Estate stamp lower right

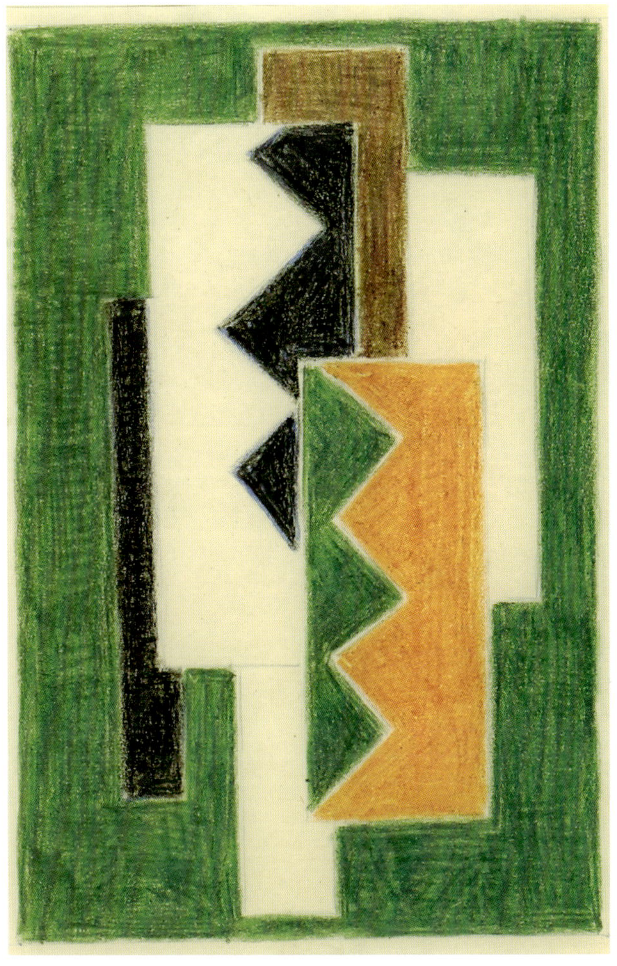

106.
Alexander Corazzo
(1908–1971)
Abstract, ca. 1940
Gouache on vellum
6 × 8 inches
Signed lower right: *Corazzo*

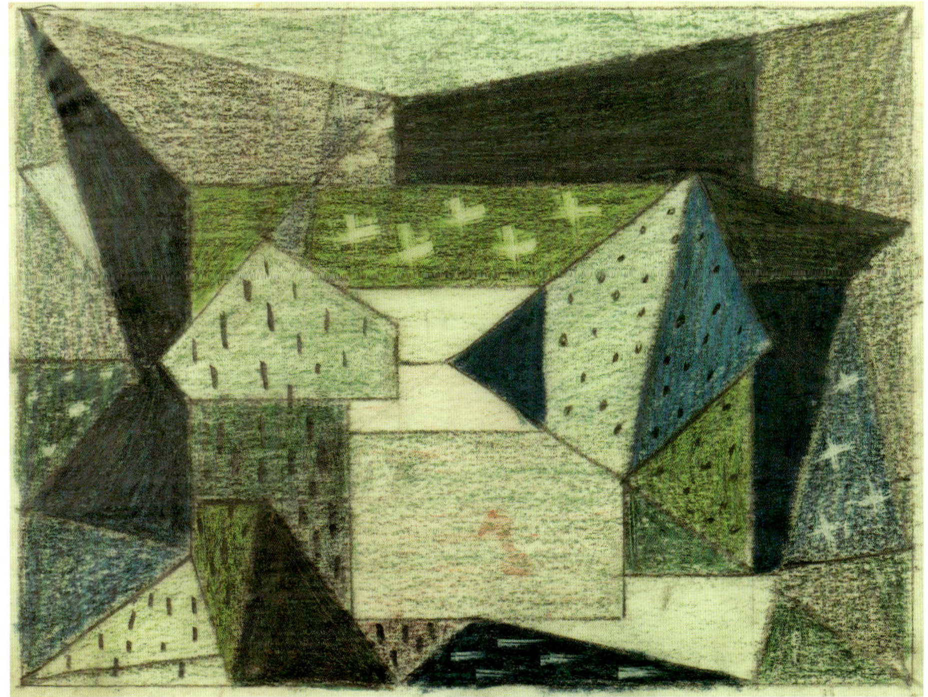

William Perkins Babcock (1826–1899)

A noted colorist who produced varied subject matter, including still lifes, figurative subjects, portraits, landscapes, and historical and mythological scenes, William Perkins Babcock was born in Boston, but lived as an expatriate in France for most of his life. In 1847 he traveled to Europe, where he was among the first Americans to study with Thomas Couture in Paris. During a stay in Barbizon, he befriended the noted painter Jean-François Millet and became inspired to produce peasant imagery in the manner of his French mentor. Though Babcock remained abroad, he exhibited frequently in the United States, showing often at the Boston Athenaeum and the Brooklyn Art Association, as well as at other venues. He also participated in the Paris Salon from 1868 to 1878. There was an active market for Babock's work in this country, and examples of it are included in many permanent collections, including the Baltimore Museum of Art and the Museum of Fine Arts, Boston. The artist died in Bois d'Arcy, France.

George Herbert Baker (1878–1943)

A noted Indiana Impressionist, George Herbert Baker specialized in landscapes in watercolor and pastel. He was born in Muncie, Indiana, and studied at the Cincinnati Art Academy. He worked during most of his career in Richmond, Indiana, where he was a member of the Richmond Group of Artists. He exhibited at the Hoosier Salon, the Richmond Palette Club, the Indiana Arts Society, and the Society of Independent Artists. A retrospective of his art was held at the Richmond Art Museum in 2001.

Donald Blagge Barton (1903–1990)

Donald Blagge Barton was a mid-twentieth-century painter of colorful Impressionist landscapes and seascapes who specialized in views of fishing boats and shacks in Gloucester and Rockport, Massachusetts. Born in Fitchburg, Massachusetts, he studied in Boston at the School of the Museum of Fine Arts and the Massachusetts Normal School. He also took private classes with Philip Leslie Hale, Gifford Beal, and William Lester Stevens. During the summers, Barton painted in Rockport and in Ogunquit, Maine, where he took classes with Henry Webster Rice and Charles Woodbury. Barton traveled in Europe and North Africa in 1926–27. The following year, he made a cross-country trip through the American South and West, where he painted Pueblo Indians and views of the Grand Canyon. With a wife and child to support, Barton had become an occupational therapist by 1935 with the Massachusetts Department of Mental Health as well as a photographer. His canvases, stored for decades in the barn of his home in Fitchburg, were rediscovered in 1987 by a Boston city planner. Shows of Barton's work were subsequently held in Boston and New Jersey, bringing him long-overdue recognition that he was able to enjoy before his death.

Robert Bates (British, b. 1943)

Gershon Benjamin (1899–1985)

A painter of cityscapes, portraits, landscapes, and still lifes, Gershon Benjamin evolved a distinctive style in which he combined a lyrical palette with simplified designs and two-dimensional shapes, achieving a subtle balance between realism and abstraction. The artist was born in Romania, but grew up in Montreal, Québec. In addition to attending art classes at the Montreal Museum of Fine Arts and the Montreal Art Association, he studied photo-engraving techniques and through this means found employment at various local newspapers. In 1923 he moved to New York, where he worked for the *Sun* and the *New York Journal American* and painted in his spare time. He also took courses at Cooper Union, the Art Students League, and the Art Alliance. During these years Benjamin associated with a circle of progressive-minded artists that included Milton Avery, Mark Rothko, Arshile Gorky, John Sloan, and Raphael and Moses Soyer, who often painted together and critiqued each other's work. He was especially close to Avery, who lived in the same studio building at Broadway and 66th Street and shared his love of gentle color harmonies. Benjamin moved to New Jersey in 1958 and two years later began painting full-time. He had his first solo exhibition at the Uptown Gallery in Manhattan in 1936 and thereafter his work appeared in numerous group shows in New York. However, Benjamin was little known to contemporary art aficionados until the early 1980s, when a series of exhibitions—at Drew University (1983) and the New Jersey Institute of Technology (1984)—brought his work before the public eye. In 2003, the exhibition *Gershon and the City* was held at Fairleigh Dickinson University in Madison, New Jersey.

Sándor Bernath (1892–1985)

A painter, illustrator, and teacher, Sándor Bernath is best known for his watercolors of sailing yachts and schooners, rendered in a clean, tight Precisionist style. He was born in Hungary. By 1918 he had moved to New York, where he was said to have studied with Edward Hopper. After at first focusing on New York City scenes, Bernath turned to painting images of ships and of the New England coastline. During the 1920s Bernath became a member of the New York Water Color Club, the American Water Color Society, and the Brooklyn Society of Modern Artists. He exhibited at the Whitney Museum of American Art and the Art Institute of Chicago. About 1927 he moved to Eastport, Maine, where he continued to live until at least 1945. His whereabouts and activities after that date are unknown.

Johann Berthelsen (1883–1972)

Johann Berthelsen was born in Copenhagan and immigrated to the United States in 1889. Initially drawn to a career in vocal music, he attended the Chicago Musical College, graduating in 1909. After touring for five years as a baritone, he joined the college's faculty, where he taught for three years, while starting to paint, encouraged by a fellow Scandinavian, Norwegian landscape painter Svend Svendsen. In 1913 Berthelsen continued to pursue a career in music, moving to Indianapolis for a position at the Indianapolis Conservatory of Music. Concurrently he pursued his interest in art, studying with the noted Indianapolis artist Wayman Adams, who had become a friend. By 1920 Berthelsen had moved to New York, where he opened his own art studio. He became fully committed to painting in 1932, specializing in scenes of New York streets and views of Central Park in the evening and winter. Accomplished in oil, pastel, and watercolor, he captured subdued tonal effects with a soft muted technique. He was a member of the American Watercolor Society and the Salmagundi Club, and he participated in the Works Progress Administration Art Program during the Great Depression.

Stanley Bielecky (1903–1985)

Stanley Bielecky was a modernist painter associated with Indiana. He was born near Berlin, Germany, and came to America with his family when he was three years old. The family settled at first in Johnstown, Pennsylvania, and then moved to the industrial city of East Chicago, Indiana—a location that provided the theme for much of Bielecky's oeuvre. Working in watercolor and oil, the artist portrayed bustling urban scenes, landscapes, and figures. After winning the Edward M. Johnson scholarship, Bielecky was able to begin his studies at the Minneapolis Institute of Arts in 1930. He continued his training at the Chicago Art Institute under George Oberteuffer and Louis Ritman. In 1938 Bielecky won a resident fellowship to the Tiffany Foundation in New York. In 1938 his work was shown at the San Francisco Museum of Art, and a few years later he exhibited at the Detroit Institute of Arts, where he won the Marjorie Beth Maxon Purchase Prize. His work was also shown at the Pennsylvania Academy of the Fine Arts, Philadelphia; the John Herron Art Institute, Indianapolis; and the Toledo Museum of Fine Arts, Ohio. Bielecky taught at the Calumet Center of Indiana University from 1937 until 1941, when he became an instructor of Fine Arts at Valparaiso Univeristy (1941–57). His teaching career was interrupted in 1942, when he served as a camofleur in the United States Army's 850th Engineer Battalion in England, France, and Germany. After the war, Bielecky resumed his teaching position at Valparaiso University, while simultaneously maintaining a studio in East Chicago.

Emil Bisttram (1895–1976)

A leader in the development of modern art in America, Emil Bisttram pioneered its introduction in the Southwest, moving from New York to Taos, New Mexico, in 1931. Before this date, the Hungarian-born artist was exposed to advanced painting and art theory through several sources. These included a close association with the Russian émigré Nicholas Roerich, whose exploration of the relationship between art and the occult contributed to the evolution of abstraction in this country. Roerich's ideas paralleled those of his famous compatriot Wassily Kandinsky, whose art and writing also influenced Bisttram. Bisttram opened his Taos School of Art (also called the Bisttram School of Fine Arts) in 1932. In 1938, along with Raymond Jonson, he founded the Transcendentalist Painting Group, whose members sought to convey the "cosmic" and "universal" by means of a nonobjective aesthetic. Yet despite his commitment to nonobjective painting, Bisttram continued to employ a range of styles throughout his career. In addition to his hard-edged, geometric abstractions, he explored Cubism, Expressionism, and representational realism.

Oscar Bluemner (1867–1938)

An important figure in American modernism, Oscar Bluemner painted expressionist landscapes informed by a variety of sources ranging from European Post-Impressionism, Asian aesthetics, and Symbolism, to the color theories of Chevreul and Goethe. Bluemner was born in Prenzlau, in Central Prussia, and studied architecture at Berlin's Königliche Technische Hochschule. He immigrated to the United States in 1892, splitting his time between Chicago and New York, before settling permanently in the latter city in 1900. In 1910 he abandoned architecture to become a painter. Dubbed "the vermilionaire" due to his preference for vivid reds and greens, Bluemner's art was inspired by the structural concerns of Paul Cézanne and cubism and the bold colorism of Vincent van Gogh. Bluemner participated in the 1913 Armory Show and in 1915 had his first American solo exhibition at Alfred Stieglitz's gallery, 291. His place among the avant-garde was affirmed in 1916, when he was included in the select group of artists whose work was featured in the *Forum Exhibition of Modern American Paintings*. While residing in New Jersey from 1916 until 1926, Bluemner drew his subjects from the regional landscape, depicting houses, barns, canals, and factories in mill towns such as Sayreville, Paterson, and Tottenville. He continued to create oils, watercolors, and caseins before moving to South Braintree, Massachusetts, where he ended his life by suicide in 1938.

Abraham J. Bogdanove (1886–1946)

Abraham J. Bogdanove was a landscape painter, portraitist, muralist, and art teacher, who is best known for his dynamic images of Monhegan Island, Maine. Born in Minsk, then part of Russia, he immigrated with his family to the United States in 1900. Settling in New York, he studied at the Cooper Union Institute of Art, the National Academy of Design, and the Columbia University School of Architecture, where he trained under the prominent mural painter Francis Davis Millet. Bogdanove created a number of important murals between 1913 and 1930, but mostly he devoted his time to landscape painting. He first visited the coast of Maine in 1915, and in 1918, he made his initial sojourn to Monhegan Island, seventeen miles off the state's mid-coast. For the rest of his life, he returned annually to Monhegan, where he purchased a home on Horn Hill and spent his days painting at the water's edge, directly recording the rocks, surf, weather-beaten fish houses, and harbor scenery. Influenced by the work of color theorist and chemist Maximilian Toch, who advocated the use of natural pigments and a limited palette, Bogdanove produced works with harmonious color schemes and permanent colors. Their strong, abstract qualities reflect the artist's responsiveness to developments in twentieth-century modernism. During the mid-1930s Bogdanove painted in Canada's Gaspé Peninsula and in Europe. From 1918 until 1942 he taught at Townsend Harris High School of the College of the City of New York (now City College of the City University of New York). Following his retirement from teaching, Bogdanove moved to Dunbarton, New Hampshire, where he died.

Frank Myers Boggs (1855–1926)

Born in Springfield, Ohio, Frank Myers Boggs grew up in New York City, where his father worked in the newspaper business. At the age of seventeen he entered the magazine world, working as a wood engraver for *Harper's*. In 1876 he went to Paris to study theater set design, but ended up instead at the Ecole des Beaux-Arts, where he received instruction and encouragement from the famous academician, Jean-Léon Gérôme. In the ensuing years Boggs painted marines and harbor scenes in Dieppe, Honfleur, and Grandcamp, as well as streetscapes, architectural subjects, and views of the Seine. Returning to the United States in 1878 or 1879, he exhibited his work at the National Academy of Design but remained a little-known figure in the art world. He subsequently returned to Paris, where his deftly rendered oils—painted in a modified impressionist style that suggests the impact of the Dutch marine artist Johann Barthold Jongkind—brought him widespread success. Boggs later made trips back to America, as well as to exotic locales such as Algiers. He exhibited his work in major international expositions in Europe as well as at the Paris Salon. Boggs, who became a French citizen in 1923, died in the town of Meudon, France. Following his death, he was awarded the prestigious French Legion of Honor.

Edward Borein (1872–1945)

Once described as a "cowpuncher translated into art," Edward Borein was one of the last of a generation of American artists to capture the romance and color of the Old West. A prolific artist, he enjoyed a long and successful career in which he documented life on the frontier in oils, etchings, and watercolors. He was born in San Leandro, California. In 1891 he enrolled at the San Francisco Art Association. After a month, he left to become a cowboy. With the sponsorship of a rancher for whom he worked, in 1897 Borein made the first of many subsequent visits to Mexico. In 1907 he moved to New York City, where he attracted a circle of friends that included the Western painter Charles Russell, as well as celebrities such as Will Rogers, Buffalo Bill Cody, and Theodore Roosevelt. Borein also established a notable reputation as an illustrator, contributing images of life in the Old West to leading magazines and newspapers, such as *Harper's Weekly* and *Collier's*, as well as *Sunset Magazine* and *Western World*. After studying etching in 1911 at the Art Students League under Vojtech Preissig and privately with the American Impressionist, Childe Hassam, he mastered the medium, going on to exhibit his graphic work at the Brooklyn Society of Etchers and at Keppel and Company in New York. Borein returned to California in 1919, settling first in Oakland and later in Santa Barbara. He continued to travel throughout his career, sojourning throughout the North and Southwest, often accompanied by his friend and fellow artist, Carl Oscar Borg. He also acted in Western movies and occasionally served as a technical director.

Simeon Braguin (1907–1997)

Born in Ukraine, Simeon Braguin and his family came to America in 1917, settling in New York City. He later took art classes at Columbia University and at the Art Students League. It was about this time that he became friendly with the Ashcan School painter William Glackens, who may have helped him organize the first solo exhibition of his paintings, held at the Marie Harriman Gallery in 1931. By 1932 Braguin had joined the staff of *Vogue* magazine. A talented draftsman, he also did illustration work for other leading magazines, such as *Saturday Evening Post* and *Mademoiselle* and produced advertisements for upscale retailers such as Saks Fifth Avenue, Bergdorf Goodman, and Bonwit Teller. Braguin was also involved with fabric and furniture design. After being appointed art director for *Vogue*, he worked closely with such celebrated photographers as Edward Steichen and Cecil Beaton. Braguin's illustrations—inspired by artists such as Paul Klee, Jean Cocteau, and Henri Matisse—were whimsical and sophisticated, distinguished by an elegant yet playful use of line. After serving in World War II, he became the art director at B. Altman's. In the late 1960s Braguin resumed painting on a regular basis, going on to evolve a highly poetic brand of abstraction that linked him with the second generation New York School. Along with his wife, the fashion editor, Janet Chatfield Taylor, he played a lively role in the art world, fraternizing with painters such as Fairfield Porter and Andy Warhol. Braguin had well-received solo exhibitions in New York City in 1971 and 1975, but in the ensuing years he worked in relative isolation, producing geometric abstractions—characterized by pastel colors and a delicate linearity—that reflected his love of sailing. A one-man show at the Yale University Art Gallery in 1991 served to re-introduce his work to contemporary audiences.

Clarence Holbrook Carter (1904–2000)

Clarence Holbrook Carter's paintings range from powerful depictions of the American Scene to evocative abstractions. Born in Portsmouth, Ohio, he studied at the Cleveland School of Art from 1923 until 1927, working under William Eastman, Henry Keller, and others. After a curator at the Cleveland Museum of Art orchestrated the sale of a number of his oils, he went to Europe, studying with Hans Hofmann in Capri and traveling throughout the Continent and Africa, where he painted landscapes and cityscapes in a precise realist manner inspired by the example of fifteenth-century Italian and Flemish painters. Returning to Cleveland in 1929, he had his first solo exhibition at the Cleveland Museum of Art and went on to teach studio classes there from 1930 to 1937. During the 1930s and 1940s, Carter painted landscapes, genre scenes, and industrial subjects depicting life in the Ohio River Valley, imbuing his work with a sense of ambiguity that set him apart from mainstream American Realism and allied him with visionary painters such as Edward Hopper and Ivan Albright. In the 1950s his work became increasingly abstract. In his late paintings he used reductive motifs, such as ovoids and mandalas, to symbolize his inner state of mind. Carter's numerous teaching posts included positions at the Carnegie Institute of Technology, Lehigh University, and the University of Iowa. In addition to many solo exhibitions, his work has been included in numerous group shows devoted to regional realism, magic realism, surrealism, and abstraction. At the time of his death, he was a resident of Milford, New Jersey.

William Chadwick (1879–1962)

A native of Dewsbury, England, William Chadwick and his family immigrated to the United States in 1882. After developing an interest in art during his boyhood, he enrolled in classes at the Art Students League of New York, working under John Henry Twachtman, Joseph DeCamp, and others. In the wake of a trip to Rome in the summer of 1901 he established his studio in Manhattan and proceeded to paint portrait and figure subjects, inspired by the example of DeCamp and James McNeill Whistler. He made his first trip to the art colony at Old Lyme, Connecticut, in 1902 and thereafter became a regular visitor. Taking his cue from older colonists such as Willard Metcalf and Walter Griffin, he eventually adopted the light palette and loose brushwork of Impressionism. In 1915 he settled permanently in Old Lyme. He continued to work in an impressionist manner long after that style had been eclipsed by modernism. In addition to Connecticut, he was active in Europe, Vermont, Bermuda, and Monhegan Island, Maine. Chadwick's studio was reconstructed on the grounds of the Florence Griswold Museum, in Old Lyme, in 1994.

Nathaniel Choate (1899–1965)

A sculptor who upheld the Beaux-Arts tradition, Nathaniel Choate was born in Southboro, Massachusetts. He began his career as a painter, studying in Paris in 1923 at the Académies Julian and Grande Chaumière. After visiting Greece in the following year, he chose to become a sculptor. To this end, he trained in Boston at the Harvard Architectural School, under John Wilson, and the Massachusetts Institute of Technology. Choate lived mostly in Europe from 1927 through 1930. From the mid-1930s onward, he resided intermittently in New York City and Phoenixville, Pennsylvania. He was a member of the National Sculpture Society, the Architectural League, and the New York Ceramic Society, and an associate member of the National Academy of Design. His work may be seen at Brookgreen Gardens, Pawleys Island, South Carolina.

Yin Yong Chun (b. 1958)

Yin Yong Chun is a contemporary Chinese painter who specializes in still lifes in which he combines a Western realist approach with Asian compositional influences. He portrays objects in meticulous detail, while synchronizing their relationships in space to produce a sense of balance and harmony. Chun is also a painter of portraits. He was born in Liaoning Province in northeast China. He studied at the China Artists' Association from 1979 to 1983 and completed his undergraduate studies in oil painting at Harbin Normal University, in the Heilongjiang Province. From 1989 until 1990 he undertook postgraduate studies at Lu Xun Academy of Fine Arts in Shenyang, Liaoning, China. During the 1980s Chun participated in local exhibitions. In the following decade he was included in several prestigious shows. He had a solo exhibition at the World Trade Center in Beijing (1993, 1994, 1996) and was included in the Beijing International Expositions (1995, 1996, 1997). Chun displayed his work in the United States for the first time in 1999, when he had a one-artist show at the World Fine Art Gallery in New York. In 2001 a joint show of his art was held at the Gallery of Graphic Arts, New York, and a solo exhibition was held at the National Arts Club, New York. In 2002 Chun participated in a group exhibition at Galerie du Monde in Hong Kong. Yin Yong Chun's works may be found in many important collections in the United States, Canada, Singapore, Taiwan, and Europe.

Frederick Stuart Church (1842–1924)

A native of Michigan who spent most of his career in New York City, Frederick Stuart Church was a creator of decorative paintings and illustrations, often of an allegorical nature that were characterized by humor and joyfulness. His works included lithe figures and animals that reveal his close study of animal anatomy. Church worked for the American Express Company in Chicago as a youth before serving in the Union artillery during the Civil War. At the conclusion of his service, he returned to Chicago and studied at the Chicago Art Academy with Walter Shirlaw. Moving to New York in 1870, he trained at the National Academy of Design with Lemuel Wilmarth and at the Art Students League. Wilmarth created illustrations for *Harper's Weekly, Frank Leslie's Weekly, Ladies Home Journal*, and *Harper's Bazaar*, among others. Church, who was elected to the National Academy of Design in 1885, showed his work there as well as at the Brooklyn Art Association, the Boston Art Club, and many other venues. His paintings were purchased by leading art collectors of his era, including Charles Lang Freer, Henry Clay Frick, and Potter Palmer.

George Clare (British, 1830–1900)

George Clare was a Victorian artist known for his highly detailed and precise fruit and flower paintings. He lived and died in Barnet, Hertfordshire, England, and spent a number of years working in Birmingham. Although little is known of his background and artistic training, his work shows the influence of the watercolorist William Henry "Bird's Nest" Hunt in his choice of subject matter and delicate, stippling technique. Clare was one of many of Hunt's followers who included John Sherrin, William Hough, and Thomas Collier. In their meticulously executed still lifes, this "school" of artists displayed the Pre-Raphaelite concern for extreme detail and truth to nature. Beginning in 1864, Clare was a regular exhibitor at the Royal Academy, the British Institution, and the Royal Society of British Artists, Suffolk Street. Birds' nests and flower blossoms on mossy banks, a favorite subject of the artist, were extremely popular with Victorian audiences. Two of Clare's three sons—Oliver and Vincent—were also artists and painted still lifes in styles comparable to those of their father.

Alson Skinner Clark (1876–1949)

Alson Skinner Clark is best known for his vivid images of the California landscape. He was born in Chicago and studied in New York at the Art Students League and with William Merritt Chase. Traveling to Paris on Chase's recommendation in 1899, he attended the Académie Julian, trained briefly under James McNeill Whistler, and exhibited at the Paris Salon in 1901. After he returned to the United States in the following year, he established his studio in Watertown, New York, where he focused on rendering winter scenes, but he also painted a wide range of subjects that he encountered during his extensive sojourns at home and abroad. In the period that followed, he painted cityscapes in his native Chicago, visited Quebec in 1906, Spain in 1909, Prague in 1912, and Dalmatia and Panama in 1913. His painting, *The Digging of the Panama Canal*, was exhibited at the 1914 Paris Salon. After World War I, in which Clark served as one of the first aerial photographers, he went to California to recover from a hearing disability incurred during the war. At first reluctant to resume his painting career, he found the desert, coast, and mountains of the southern California landscape too fascinating to resist. Forsaking his earlier style of small, intimate and at times somber compositions, he began working on large plein-air landscapes in a looser, brighter mode, which eventually expanded into murals. These full-scale wall decorations were so successful that the artist received commissions for them until the end of his life. In 1922 Clark joined Guy Rose, a colleague from his days in Paris, to found the Stickney Art School in Pasadena. With the exception of three trips to Mexico and one to Europe in 1936, the artist remained in southern California until his death in 1949.

Walter Clark (1848–1917)

Walter Clark was a highly respected landscape painter as well as a sculptor. A native of Brooklyn, Clark initially studied engineering at the Massachusetts Institute of Technology before touring Europe, India, China, and Japan in 1869. He later attended the National Academy of Design in New York and studied drawing with Lemuel Wilmarth and sculpture with J. Scott Hartley. Clark began to favor painting after executing a number of portrait busts and works in terracotta. His early landscapes were Tonalist in spirit and emphasized mood and feeling, a style indebted to George Inness, whose studio was adjacent to Clark's in New York City. In the late 1890s he became increasingly influenced by the American Impressionists, and his friends included painters Edward Potthast, John

Henry Twachtman, and Joseph DeCamp. Clark earned a number of important awards, including silver medals at two international expositions and the coveted Inness Gold Medal from the National Academy in 1902. Clark was the father of the painter and artist-biographer Eliot Candee Clark.

Colin Campbell Cooper (1856–1937)

An Impressionist painter of oils and watercolors, Colin Campbell Cooper is best known for urban scenes, landscapes, and images of architectural structures that are notable for their able draftsmanship, sparkling color, and ability to capture the character of their sites. Born in Philadelphia, Cooper studied at the Pennsylvania Academy of the Fine Arts with Thomas Eakins and in Paris at the Académie Julian and the Ecole Delecluse. By 1895 Cooper had returned to Philadelphia, where he taught watercolor classes at the Drexel Institute. In 1902 he moved to New York and began to paint scenes of the city's dramatic skylines, focusing on its new skyscrapers. He also painted scenes on sojourns abroad to Europe and Asia. Cooper made his first trip to California in 1915, when he was invited to exhibit work at the Panama-Pacific Exposition in San Francisco. In 1921 he moved to Santa Barbara, California, where he became the dean of the School of Painting at the Santa Barbara School for the Arts and painted light-filled images of houses and gardens near his new home.

Alexander Corazzo (1908–1971)

Born in Lyon, France, Alexander Corazzo was a noted artist and architect. Gifted in music, he enrolled in 1918 in the National Conservatory of Music in Lyon. He went on to study civil engineering, but in 1927 he immigrated to the United States, settling in Minnesota. There he attended the School of Art in St. Paul from 1929 to 1934. Soon he developed a modernist approach influenced by Cubism, Constructivism, and geometric abstraction. In 1935 he was invited to join Abstract-Création, a European group of important avant-garde artists that included Mondrian, Léger, Jean Arp, Robert Delaunay, Gino Severini, Edvard Munch, and Wassily Kandinsky. Along with Carl Holty and Alexander Calder, he was one of few Americans invited to join this group. In 1937 Corazzo attended the first classes of the New Bauhaus School in Chicago that was established by the experimental artist, painter and sculptor, László Moholy-Nagy. He left the school only a year later to protest its growing emphasis on design over painting. Corazzo continued to paint and exhibit his work widely, participating in group shows at the Metropolitan Museum of Art, New York; the National Gallery of Art, Washington, D.C.; the Art Institute of Chicago; and the Whitney Museum of American Art, New York; among others. In 1941 he joined the American Abstract Artists. The following year he was honored with a one-man exhibition at the San Francisco Museum of Art and again in 1943 at the Santa Barbara Museum of Art. During the 1940s Corazzo became more interested in architecture and enrolled in the Illinois Institute of Technology where he studied with Mies van der Rohe. He was awarded an architecture degree in 1946 and went on to practice in that field until his death in 1971.

Eugene Dana (1912–1987)

A noted educator, painter, designer, and filmmaker, Eugene Dana was born in Marengo, Illinois. After receiving a bachelor's degree from the University of Wisconsin, he went on to study at the St. Paul School of Arts in Minnesota and at the University of Michigan. His teachers during these years included Cameron Booth and Leroy Turner, as well as Josef Albers, an influential abstract painter and theoretician who helped introduce Bauhaus principles of art and design into American art circles. Dana served as head of the art department at Drake University in Des Moines, Iowa, during 1945–46 and taught at Brooklyn College during 1946–47. In 1947 he became an associate professor at the Illinois Institute of Technology in Chicago, where he taught classes in graphic design. During the 1930s and 1940s, he exhibited his work at venues throughout the Midwest. He spent his later years painting rhythmic geometric abstractions that reveal his interest in two-dimensional forms and prismatic colors and reflect the impact of his early contact with progressive-minded artists such as Albers.

Harold Christopher Davies
(1891–1976)

A modernist artist best known for works in the Abstract Expressionist style, Harold Christopher Davies was born in Seattle and grew up on a farm near Cherrydale, Virginia. He began to study art at age fourteen, when he attended the Corcoran Art School, Washington, D.C. He moved in 1909 to Fresno, California, where he found employment as a clerk for the San Joaquin Power & Light Company. In 1912 and again in 1920 he studied at the San Francisco Institute of Art. He continued to paint even after moving to Oakland in 1921, where he worked for a metal products company and became president in 1933 of the California Spray Chemical Company. His work as a successful executive necessitated moves to Huntsville, Alabama (1945–57) and then to Long Island, where he found time to associate with Adolph Gottlieb, Franz Kline, and Willem de Kooning. After his retirement in 1969 he returned to California, establishing the home and studio in Inverness on Tomales Bay where he resided for the rest of his life. He was a member of the Oakland Art League, the San Francisco Art Association, and the Huntsville Art Association.

Charles Harold Davis (1856–1933)

The Tonalist landscape painter Charles Harold Davis was born in Amesbury, Massachusetts. Not planning to become an artist, he left school to work in a carriage factory. It was only after seeing an exhibition of landscapes by Jean-François Millet that he decided to study drawing. He enrolled at the School of the Museum of Fine Arts, Boston, where he received instruction from Otto Grundman. From 1880 to 1881 he furthered his training in Paris at the Académie Julian in the atelier of Jules Joseph Lefebvre and Gustave Boulanger. During the decade that followed, Davis remained in France, residing in Paris and making frequent visits to the Barbizon and Fontainebleau regions of France, where he painted the rural subject matter that would be his focus throughout the rest of his career. After returning to the United States, Davis settled in Mystic, Connecticut, where he lived until the end of his life. In his early works, Davis employed subdued tones and the soft glazes typical of Barbizon School art. About 1895 he began to focus on the subject of clouds, which he portrayed in different atmospheric and weather conditions. He was considered one of the finest painters among the Tonalists, and was especially esteemed for his ability to express subtleties of color and form. In the course of his career, Davis received many awards, including a silver medal at the Paris Universal Exposition of 1889. He became a member of the National Academy of Design in 1903.

Terry DeLapp (b. 1934)

A perceptive observer of his environment, Terry DeLapp is a modern-day Tonalist, recognized for his evocative depictions of the central coast of California. His choice of motifs—the farms and ranches of the Salinas and San Joaquin valleys, the green hills of Cambria and San Simeon, and the luxuriant flora of the region—reveals, as he puts it, his "love and concern for the land and what is on it." Born in Pasadena, DeLapp studied at the Chouinards Art Academy in Hollywood and at the University of California. From 1959 to 1992 he operated the Terry DeLapp Gallery in Los Angeles, the first gallery on the West coast to showcase nineteenth-century American art. DeLapp currently lives and works in Cambria, California. He has been exhibiting his paintings since the early 1980s, participating in group shows in California, New Mexico, and elsewhere. DeLapp has had numerous solo exhibitions as well, at the Bakersfield Museum of Art, California (1998) and Spanierman Gallery, New York (2001).

Charles Warren Eaton (1857–1937)

A major figure in the American Tonalist movement, Charles Warren Eaton painted evocative landscapes in New Jersey, New England, and Europe. Guided by his desire to convey the underlying moods of nature, he eschewed grandiose vistas in favor of quieter, more intimate views, which he depicted at dawn or dusk. He studied in New York at the National Academy of Design and at the Art Students League. The most important influence on him was the Barbizon-style art of George Inness, whom he met in 1889. Eaton established a summer residence in Bloomfield, New Jersey, in 1887 and spent the next decade depicting the local countryside during the late autumn and winter. After 1900 he made seasonal visits to Thompson and Colebrook, Connecticut, where he developed his signature theme—a grove of pine trees silhouetted against a sunset or moonlit skies. Eaton was also active in Belgium, Italy, and Glacier Park, Montana.

Henry Farrer (1843–1903)

Henry Farrer was an important American Pre-Raphaelite artist, well known for landscapes and still lifes in watercolor, oil, and etching. He was the younger brother of Thomas Charles Farrer, the foremost champion of the aesthetic dogma of John Ruskin in America at mid-century. Following the lead of his brother, who first came to the United States in the late 1850s, Henry Farrer immigrated to this country at age nineteen and established a studio in New York. By the late 1860s he was espousing Ruskinian principles, which are evident in his meticulous watercolor studies of fruits and flowers. Part of a wave of American artists dedicated to exploring the watercolor medium in the 1860s, Farrer was a founder in 1866 of the American Society of Painters in Water Color. In 1877 he participated in the founding of the New York Etching Club and became the president of this organization in 1881. Farrer established a studio in New York's Tenth Street Studio Building in the 1880s. The influence of other residents of this prominent artists' building, such as William Merritt Chase, may have encouraged him to develop a more painterly style. From about 1887 until his death in 1903, Farrer lived in Brooklyn.

Isabelle H. Ferry (1865–1937)

An Impressionist painter who specialized in views of landscapes and gardens, Isabelle H. Ferry was born in Williamsburg, Massachusetts. She studied in Paris with Adolphe William Bouguereau, Charles Boutet de Monvel, and Tony Robert-Fleury. On her return to the United States, she took classes in New York with the Tonalist painter Dwight William Tryon and the important realist Robert Henri. By 1897 Ferry had returned to Massachusetts, settling in Easthampton, near her hometown. She summered in Boothbay Harbor, Maine, where she maintained a studio, taught art classes, and became an active figure in the art scene. Ferry developed a style that included thick impastoed surfaces and a use of vivid colors. Her subjects included the cottages, gardens, and bays of New England, which she portrayed in idealized terms.

Frances Foy (1890–1963)

Active in her native Chicago in the early twentieth century, Frances Foy was a realist painter known especially for floral still lifes and portraits. She studied at the Chicago Academy of Arts (later the Art Institute of Chicago), under Fred Schook and J. Wellington Reynolds. She also trained with George Bellows and Randall Davey when they were visiting instructors at the academy. Foy married the artist Gustav Dahstrom in 1923. After a trip to Europe in 1928, Foy created a number of works revealing evidence of her exploration of a variety of modernist styles, including cubism. Foy was a member of a group of Chicago artists called the Ten and participated as a WPA muralist, creating a mural for the Chestnut Street Postal Station in Chicago. She belonged to the Chicago Society of Artists, receiving medals there and for works exhibited at the Art Institute of Chicago.

Frederick Frieseke (1874–1939)

The leading American Impressionist working in Giverny, France, during the early 1900s, Frederick Frieseke won international acclaim for his colorful, light-filled portrayals of the female figure. His signature style—which served as the dominant aesthetic in Giverny for well over a decade—was based on the synthesis of Impressionist light, color, and subject matter with the decorative aspects of Post-Impressionism. Frieseke was born in Owosso, Michigan. After studying at the Art Institute of Chicago and the Art Students League of New York, he went to Paris in 1898, resuming his training at the Académie Julian and at the Académie Carmen, where he was taught by James McNeill Whistler. During the early 1900s he depicted women in sparsely furnished interiors, working in a Tonalist style reminiscent of Whistler's. In 1906 he took a house in Giverny, not far from where Claude Monet lived. There Frieseke combined the bright palette and loose brushwork of Impressionism with the rich patterning favored by Nabis painters such as Edouard Vuillard and Pierre Bonnard. His portrayals of women in intimate domestic settings and in sunlit flower gardens won him acclaim, both in Europe and the United States, and inspired other members of the American Givernois, among them Richard Miller, Karl Anderson, and Louis Ritman. In 1919, Frieseke moved to Le Mesnil-sur-Blangy, where he remained until his death. During his later years he continued to paint the female figure and produced many portraits, imbuing his work with a greater sense of realism.

Joseph Garlock (1884–1980)

Born near Minsk, then part of Russia, Joseph Garlock immigrated to New York City in 1906 and settled in Bloomsfield, New Jersey, where he raised a family and operated a number of businesses, including a fruit and vegetable stand and a line of commuter buses, which was eventually taken over by the New Jersey public bus service. On his retirement at the age of sixty-five, Garlock spent a summer in Woodstock, New York, where he began to paint. He went on to work prolifically in Woodstock and New Jersey until 1965, when a physical palsy in his hands prevented him from continuing his career. Rendered in a simplified realist style similar to that of Milton Avery, Garlock's work, consisting of paintings and sculptures, expresses his personal interpretations of his subjects. Often mixing imagined elements into his art, he painted motifs that ranged widely, including religious ceremonies from his childhood in Russia, views of Woodstock, New York City, and the New Jersey shore. Garlock kept his activity as a painter in privacy, storing his works in a private room on his Woodstock residence. It was not until 1999 that his art was rediscovered and began to be shown to the public.

William Glackens (1870–1938)

A key member of the New York Realists active in the early twentieth century, William Glackens hailed from Philadelphia, where he attended classes at the Pennsylvania Academy of the Fine Arts. He worked as an artist-reporter until 1895, when he made a trip to Europe with his friend and fellow artist, Robert Henri. One year later, he relocated to New York City and became a successful illustrator for the *New York Herald* and the *World*, as well as leading magazines such as *McClure's* and *Harper's Bazaar*. It was about this time that he took up easel painting, focusing his attention on objective, unsentimentalized depictions of urban life that revealed his keen powers of observation. In 1908, along with the painters Henri, John Sloan, Everett Shinn, and others, Glackens exhibited in the landmark exhibition of the Eight held at the Macbeth Gallery in New York, an event that represented an important challenge to mainstream academic art. By 1910 he had abandoned his low-keyed palette and robust realism in favor of the soft feathery brushwork and vibrant hues associated with the Impressionism of Pierre-Auguste Renoir. Later in his career, the artist moved away from contemporary subjects in favor of portraits, figural subjects, and still lifes. Throughout his career, Glackens exhibited widely, winning awards for both his paintings and illustrations. He died in Westport, Connecticut.

Arthur Clifton Goodwin (1864–1929)

A native of Portsmouth, New Hampshire, Arthur Clifton Goodwin was a relative latecomer to art when he began to paint about 1900. Although he was largely self-taught, Goodwin closely studied the art of the American Impressionists and Ashcan School painters. On his own, he began to work primarily in oil and pastel, developing an Impressionist style characterized by vigorous, sketchy brushwork and a vibrant, high-keyed palette. Gradually his lively, colorful renderings of Boston's parks, docks, and plazas attracted a steady clientele. In 1921 he moved to New York, where he rented a studio on Washington Square and developed a reputation as one of the few American Impressionists to prefer urban subjects. His views of New York's avenues, bridges, and parks are memorable for their imaginative designs and glowing light. The artist and his wife later moved to a farm in Chatham, New York, an area that inspired many of Goodwin's picturesque landscape views.

Arshile Gorky (1904–1948)

A leading Abstract Expressionist, Arshile Gorky was born Vosdanig Manoog Adoian in a small village in Armenia. During the First World War his family was uprooted, his father and sisters escaping to America, while Gorky, his mother and a sister became refugees in Russia. In 1919, after his mother died of starvation, the artist made his way to the United States, where he changed his name to Arshile Gorky. He went on to study at the Rhode Island School of Design, the New School of Design in Boston, and Grand Central School of Art in New York. His earliest paintings show the influence of Paul Cézanne and the later works of Pablo Picasso. By the 1940s, inspired by painters such as Roberto Matta, he was incorporating elements of Surrealism into his work, imbuing his paintings with metaphoric, botanical, and sexual symbols that became increasingly personal in tone. His later years were marked by tragedy, including the loss of much of his oeuvre in a 1946 studio fire, a bout of cancer, an automobile accident that left his painting arm paralyzed, and the breakdown of his marriage. He committed suicide in Sherman, Connecticut, in July of 1948.

Aaron Harry Gorson (1872–1933)

Aaron Harry Gorson was a pioneering painter of the American industrial landscape in the late nineteenth and early twentieth centuries. Unlike the later Precisionists, who focused on the abstract forms of industry, Gorson celebrated the sheer spectacle and physical beauty that he discovered in this subject. He was born in Kovno (Kaunas) in Lithuania and came to America in 1888, joining his brother in Philadelphia. There he worked as a machine operator in a clothing factory while taking night classes in art, first at the Spring Garden Institute and later at the Pennsylvania Academy of the Fine Arts, where he studied with Thomas Anshutz, whose realist style he quickly emulated. Gorson traveled to Paris about 1900 and attended the Académies Julian and Colarossi, studying under Jean Paul Laurens and Benjamin Constant. He became intrigued by James McNeill Whistler's art, which inspired many of his later landscape scenes of twilight,

early morning, night, and foggy days that he frequently entitled *Nocturne* or *Prelude*. Returning to Philadelphia in 1902, Gorson was soon drawn to Pittsburgh by lucrative portrait commissions, but Pittsburgh's industrial steel mills ultimately proved his preferred subject. Working in a realist mode with subtle Impressionist inflections, Gorson spent the next eighteen years painting these sprawling mills, often depicting them in night scenes that emphasized dramatic lighting and atmospheric effects. In 1921 the artist moved to New York, where he lived and painted for the rest of his life.

John Graham (1886–1961)

Born in Kiev, John Graham is best known for the Cubist-influenced, thickly painted works he created in the 1930s as well as for his role as an important promoter of modern art and avant-garde theory in America from the late 1920s through the early 1940s. The son of noble Polish expatriate parents living in Russia, Graham was born as Ivan Gratianovitch Dombrovski. On receiving a law degree, he was employed by the Czarist regime and served as a second lieutenant in Grand Duke Michael's Circassian Regiment. However, because of his later involvement in counterrevolutionary activities, he was imprisoned by the Bolsheviks. Eventually he escaped to Poland, and in 1920 he arrived in New York. He subsequently changed his name to John, the English equivalent of Ivan, and he chose Graham as his surname, as it was similar to the Cyrillic spelling of Dombrovski. Turning to art full-time, Graham studied from 1922 to 1924 at the Art Students League, where he befriended John Sloan. During the mid-1920s, he traveled extensively in Europe, serving as an important conduit for the exchange of ideas between the continents. After becoming an American citizen in 1927, he settled in Baltimore, where his art attracted the attention of Duncan Phillips, who had established the Phillips Memorial Gallery (now the Phillips Collection) in 1920. A one-man show of Graham's work was held at Phillips in 1929 and in the same year at the Dudensing Gallery in New York. Graham had two solo exhibitions in Paris, in 1928 and 1930. Although his purely abstract paintings of the 1930s were destroyed, Graham produced a significant body of graceful and witty works that reveal the influence of Picasso as well as of synthetic cubism. In addition to his career as an artist, Graham was a critic, dealer, patron, promoter, and educator. He was especially knowledgeable about Italian Renaissance bronzes and African sculpture. In 1937 he published *System and Dialectics of Art*, a treatise on art and philosophy constructed as a lengthy Socratic dialogue. A significant figure in the development of Abstract Expressionism, Graham was closely associated with Arshile Gorky, David Smith, and Willem de Kooning in the late 1930s. In 1942 Graham organized the exhibition that first seriously presented the work of Jackson Pollock. Denouncing Picasso and abstract art in the 1940s, Graham turned away from the art world to produce synthetic works that reflected his love of the Italian Renaissance and were embellished with private symbols.

Marie Henrietta Osthaus Griffith

(1855–1927)

A specialist in floral landscapes painted with vigorous strokes of color, Marie Henrietta Osthaus Griffith was a prominent Impressionist painter associated with in Toledo, Ohio, at the turn of the twentieth century. She was born in Wohldenberg, Hanover, Prussia, and was the sister Edmund Henry Osthaus, a prominent painter of hunting dogs. She immigrated with her family to America in 1885, settling in Oshkosh, Wisconsin. In 1888 she moved to Toledo, Ohio, and began to teach at the Toledo Blade Art School, where her brother Edmund had become director two years earlier. In the years that followed, Griffith raised five children, but continued to paint and take an active role in the Toledo art scene. She was a charter member and vice president of the Athena Society in Toledo, an organization of women artists, and taught for many years at St. Ursula's Academy and Art School, a boarding and day school for girls. She was a member of the Society of Western Artists and the National Society of Associated Artists. She exhibited at the Toledo Art Museum, which included many of Griffith's works in a retrospective of the Athena Society held in 1973.

Oliver Dennett Grover (1861–1927)

Oliver Dennett Grover was born and raised in Earlville, Illinois, seventy-five miles west of Chicago. He studied law at the University of Chicago and art at the Chicago Academy of Design. Supported by an endowment from his family, at the age of eighteen, he gave up law to go to Europe. He trained in Munich at the Royal Academy (1879), in Florence with Frank Duveneck (1880), and in Paris at the Académie Julian (1884). He traveled abroad many times in the course of his career, but after 1885 his base was Chicago. There he painted portraits and landscapes and produced decorative designs, including murals for the Chicago World's Exposition (1893), the Branford Memorial Library, Connecticut (1896), and the Blackstone Memorial Library, Chicago (1903). The artist taught at the School of the Art Institute of Chicago (1887–92) and was an organizer and president of the Society of Chicago Artists and of the Society of Western Artists.

Charles Harry Humphriss (1867–1964)

Born in England, Charles Harry Humphriss was a sculptor of naturalistic bronzes who specialized in portraying Native American subjects that express the peaceful nature, humanity, and dignity of his subjects. He also rendered sculptures of soldiers, cowboys, animal figures, reliefs, decorative panels, monuments, fountains, and architectural elements for buildings. Humphriss studied woodcarving in London under the Victorian artist Thomas H. Kendall before immigrating in 1890 to America. There he settled in New York, but frequently traveled to the West in search of inspiration for his work. Some of his best-known works show his subjects engaged in prayer, including *Appeal to the Great Spirit* (1900; Gilcrease Museum, Tulsa, Oklahoma) and *Indian's Appeal to Manitou* (1906; Gilcrease Museum, Tulsa, Oklahoma). Humphriss exhibited at the National Academy of Design, the Pennsylvania Academy of the Fine Arts, and the Art Institute of Chicago. He was a member of the National Sculpture Society and of the Society of Independent Artists, with which he exhibited in 1917 and 1918. About 1923 Humphriss executed decorative stone work for the Biltmore Hotel in Los Angeles and the Cadet Hospital in West Point, New York. The following year he produced similar carvings for the Biltmore Hotel in Atlanta, Georgia.

Charles Salis Kaelin (1858–1929)

Described as an artist whose "love of nature amounted to a passion," Charles Salis Kaelin was a respected member of the artists' colony at Rockport, Massachusetts, during the early twentieth century. The son of a Swiss lithographer, he began his formal training in his hometown of Cincinnati, studying at the McMicken School of Design and privately under John Henry Twachtman. Moving to New York in 1879, he continued his studies at the Art Students League and then worked as a lithographer. Back in Cincinnati, in 1892 he joined the prestigious Strobridge Lithography Company as a designer of theater posters and calendars and spent his free time on sketching trips to southern Ohio and Kentucky, where he created delicate pastel landscapes in the poetic manner of Twachtman. Kaelin first visited Gloucester, Massachusetts, on the Cape Ann peninsula in 1900 and made seasonal trips there, until he settled permanently in the nearby town of Rockport in 1916. About this time he evolved an advanced Divisionist technique—rooted in European Post-Impressionism—wherein emphatic strokes of crayon or oil paint are tightly woven together to create an intricate tapestry of line and color. He applied this method, deemed "daring" and "experimental" by contemporary critics, to his many depictions of the harbors, coastlines, and woodlands of Cape Ann.

Otis Kaye (1885–1974)

Best known for his images of American currency, Otis Kaye continued the trompe l'oeil tradition of William Harnett, John Haberle, and John Frederick Peto well into the twentieth century. A master of visual illusion, Kaye was known for his technical virtuosity and his highly inventive compositions. He was fond of the visual pun: many of Kaye's money pictures from the 1920s and 1930s include humorous references to the economic and social eccentricities of the era as well as to the paintings by trompe l'oeil artists who preceded him. Kaye was born in Neemah, Michigan, and moved to New York in 1904. There he attended the New York School of Art and came into contact with Nicholas Alden Brooks, a noted still life painter whose depictions of money, playbills, and posters would influence Kaye's own thematic preferences. From 1905 until 1914, Kaye lived in Germany, where he studied engineering and created delicate drawings of figures, animals, and insects. After returning to the United States, he settled in Pittsburgh until the mid-1920s, during which time he familiarized himself with the still lifes of Harnett. So inspired, he began painting depictions of currency in his spare time, working in the precise, highly detailed manner associated with the trompe l'oeil tradition. After about 1930 Kaye expanded his thematic repertoire to include other trompe l'oeil motifs, such as firearms and musical instruments. He also began to paint the figure and taught himself etching techniques by copying prints by Rembrandt and Whistler, always signing them with his own name. Kaye continued to paint, draw, and etch throughout the 1950s and 1960s, depicting money, paper oddities, and monumental figure compositions and landscapes. Kaye's wife and daughter died in a tragic car accident in the 1950s; about the same time, his son moved to Europe, virtually disappearing from sight. After making a short trip to New York in the spring of 1969, Kaye went to Dresden, possibly in search of his son and remained there until his death in 1974.

Louis Aston Knight (1873–1948)

Louis Aston Knight was an avid outdoor painter who took great delight in depicting the fast-flowing rivers and streams of Normandy. Inspired by both the Impressionist and realist traditions, he created lyrical images replete with water effects and outdoor light that reflect his belief that "Nature is beautiful enough to inspire masterpieces to those who are willing to copy it and to give to others the poetical effect nature expresses." Born in Paris, Knight was the son of the American expatriate painter Daniel Ridgway Knight. In addition to studying under his father, he attended classes at the Académie Julian from 1891 to 1898. His earliest landscapes were created in Normandy and Brittany and along the Seine, near Paris. He later worked in and around his country home at Beaumont-le-Roger, which he purchased in 1920. Prior to moving permanently to New York in 1940, Knight made lengthy visits to the United States, exhibiting in New York and Philadelphia and painting landscapes in Maine, Connecticut, and elsewhere in the Northeast. He won many awards and honors in France and the United States. His popularity in America was much enhanced in 1922, when President Warren G. Harding purchased one of his paintings for the White House. Knight was also active in Venice (1907–13), England (1911–13), California (1930), and Jamaica (1936).

Yasuo Kuniyoshi (1893–1953)

One of the leading members of the Woodstock art colony, Yasuo Kuniyoshi was born in Okayama, Japan. He came to America in 1906 and went on to study at the Los Angeles School of Art. In 1910 he moved to New York City, where he resumed his training at the National Academy of Design, the Independent School of Art, and the Art Students League. He made his first visit to Woodstock, New York in 1918, painting landscapes under the auspices of the League's summer school. Following this, he went on to spend several summers in Ogunquit, Maine under the patronage of the publisher and art collector, Hamilton Easter Field. By the early 1920s Kuniyoshi had developed a distinctive aesthetic in which he synthesized aspects of Japanese art, folk art, and modernism with a sense of humor and a dream-like fantasy that was uniquely his own. He later painted still lifes and depictions of solitary women inspired by the example of a fellow artist, Jules Pascin. Kuniyoshi's oeuvre includes lithographs and photographs, too. His late work became more serious in tone, reflecting the sadness he felt during World War II , when Japanese people living in the United States were viewed as enemies. The artist, who died in New York City, is represented in major public collections throughout the United States.

Fletcher Martin (1904–1979)

One of the finest figure painters to emerge during the Depression Era, Fletcher Martin drew his subjects from the American Scene, exploring subjects such as boxers locked in combat and drunken habitués of saloons to cowboys, baseball players, and women. Martin combined his concern for rendering contemporary daily life with his own uncanny insight into the human qualities of his subjects; accordingly, the cast of characters that populate his paintings display a range of emotions, moods, and experiences. The artist's style was rooted in the realist tradition, although he also frequently incorporated modernist principles of abstraction into his work. Born in Palisade, Colorado, Martin began drawing and painting while serving in the Navy (1922–26). He later settled in Los Angeles, where he worked for a printing company while pursuing his artistic interests in his spare time. During the early 1930s he was an assistant to the Mexican muralist David Siquieros. In 1936 he quit his printing job and worked as a WPA artist, executing murals for public buildings in California, Texas, and Idaho. In 1938 he joined the faculty at the Art Center School in Los Angeles. For the next three decades he taught at many prestigious institutions in the United States, while continuing his activity as a painter. Martin also illustrated several books, and in 1943 traveled to North Africa as an artist/war correspondent for *Life* magazine.

Giovanni Martino (1908–1998)

Giovanni Martino received his training in his hometown of Philadelphia, attending classes at the La France Art Institute, the Philadelphia Graphic Sketch Club, and the

Pennsylvania Academy of the Fine Arts during the 1920s. He also received instruction from his older brother, Frank, who operated the Martino Studios, a commercial art firm in Philadelphia. Following the example of his sibling, and another brother, Antonio, who was also a painter, Martino went on to specialize in views of regional scenery, working in and around Manayunk and New Hope, Pennsylvania. His style was essentially realistic, but his keen sense of design and his method of conceiving architectural forms as flat, planar shapes demonstrate the impact of modern styles such as cubism and abstraction. During a long and successful career, Martino won many awards and honors, including election as an academician at the National Academy of Design (1944). His wife, Eva, is an artist, as are his daughters, Nina and Babette.

Louisa Matthiasdottir (1917–2000)

The Icelandic-born artist Louisa Matthiasdottir is best known for her brightly colored still lifes, portraits, and landscapes. Born in Reykjavik, she studied in Denmark and in Paris with Marcel Gromaire, before immigrating to the United States in 1943. Matthiasdottir settled in New York and studied at the Hans Hoffman School. In 1944 she married fellow artist Leland Bell. Matthiasdottir's first solo show, which was at the artists' cooperative Jane Street Gallery, was in 1948. Over the course of her career, she exhibited in solo and group exhibitions in galleries and museums around the country, including in the Whitney Museum of American Art's biennial exhibition in 1973. Matthiasdottir died in Delhi, New York.

Helen Charlton McClain

(b. 1887–active 1940)

Helen Charlton McClain was a painter of portraits and landscapes, including urban scenes rendered in the style of the Ashcan School. She was born in Toronto, Canada, and studied at the New York School of Fine and Applied Art under Kenneth Hayes Miller and R. Sloan Bredin. She was a member of the National Association of Women Painters and Sculptors, the Ontario Society of Artists, and the Helconian Club, Toronto. By 1929 she had left New York to return to Toronto, where she continued to paint and exhibit her work.

Pierre Jules Mène (French, 1810–1879)

A popular and successful French animalier sculptor, Pierre Jules Mène was best known for his bronzes of animals that often romanticized his subjects. He was drawn in particular to domestic animals, featuring dogs and horses, frequently engaged in hunting. Born in Paris, Mène was largely self-taught and earned his living by producing metalwork to be used for furniture ornaments and clock decorations. He gained his expertise by drawing

animals at the Jardin des Plantes in Paris. In 1837 he established the first of many foundries, where he would cast his bronzes throughout his career, creating works that were of the highest quality in their detail and workmanship and that were produced with variety of patinas. Mène first achieved success when a bronze sculpture of a dog and fox that he had made were exhibited at the Paris Salon. He would continue to show at the Salon in the years ahead, and received first class medals at the London exhibitions of 1855 and 1861. In 1861 he was awarded the Cross of the Legion d'Honneur. After Mène's death, his foundry was run by his son in law, Auguste Cain, who continued to produce his own works as well as those of Mène. In 1892 after Cain's death, Susse Fréres took over the foundry and published a complete catalogue of Mène's works, which they continued to sell with their own foundry mark and seal.

James Arthur Merriam (1880–1951)

A painter of landscapes, James Arthur Merriam established a notable reputation for his colorful depictions of southern California. Like many artists associated with California's plein-air tradition, he began his career elsewhere in the United States. Merriam was born in Canada. By age seventeen he was working as an artist in Detroit, remaining there until the early 1900s. In 1920 he moved permanently to Los Angeles. Soon, he developed a passion for Western terrain, going on to capture the special qualities of the light and landscape with directness and spontaneity. Merriam spent the ensuing years painting Impressionist-inspired views of California's magnificent scenery—its coastline, canyons, missions, distinctive flora, arid deserts, and snowcapped mountains.

Henry Hobart Nichols (1869–1962)

Known for oil paintings, pastels, and watercolors of quiet subdued landscapes, Henry Hobart Nichols was a specialist in snow scenes and images of hazy, atmospheric days in wooded countrysides. He was born in Washington, D.C., and began his studies in his native city under Howard Helmick. He continued his training at the Art Students League in New York and later traveled to Paris, where he enrolled at the Académie Julian and received instruction from Claudio Castellucho. After returning to the United States, Nichols settled in New York City. He lived in Manhattan until 1910, when he moved to the New York suburb of Bronxville. He found most of his subjects near his Bronxville home and at other locations in New York State and in New England. Hobart was actively involved in many art organizations throughout his career and was particularly devoted to promoting and supporting his fellow artists. He was assistant director to the United States Fine Arts Division at the Paris Exposition of 1900. In 1912 he was elected an associate at the National Academy of Design; he became an Academician in 1920, and served as the Academy's president from 1939 to 1949. He was a member of the Society of Washington Artists, the Washington Water Color Club, the New York Water Color Club, the National Arts Club, the Allied Artists of America, the Lotos Club, the Cosmos Club, the Century Club, and the North Shore Arts Association. Nichols received many prizes and awards from the National Academy of Design, the Society of Washington Artists, and the Corcoran Gallery of Art.

Robert H. Nisbet (1879–1961)

The leading painter in Kent, Connecticut, during the early twentieth century, Robert Nisbet was recognized for his "keen…perception of elusive and intangible moods" and for his thorough command of technique. In addition to painting poetic landscapes and seascapes, he was a gifted etcher whose work was widely collected during his day. Nisbet studied at the Rhode Island School of Design in his native Providence and at the Art Students League in New York. After further study and travel in Europe, he moved to Manhattan in 1907, remaining there until 1911, when he settled in South Kent. He depicted the local countryside in all seasons, favoring compositions with distinctive groupings of trees. He also painted views of rivers, brooks, and the sea, working in a style that conjoined Impressionist strategies of light and color with the decorative concerns of Post-Impressionism. He exhibited regularly in New York, Philadelphia, Chicago, and elsewhere, winning many awards and honors. He was a member and one-time president of the Kent Art Association.

Bror Julius Olsson Nordfeldt
(1878–1955)

A painter and printmaker who played a notable role in the development of American Modernism outside of New York City, Nordfeldt was born Bror Julius Olsson in Tullstrop, Sweden. His family later settled in Chicago, where, in 1899, Nordfeldt took classes at Art Institute of Chicago and assisted Albert Herter in executing a mural commission for the Paris Exposition. In 1900 he traveled to the French capital, training briefly at the Académie Julian before opening his own atelier. He also studied woodblock printing with Frank Morley Fletcher in London. Three years later Nordfeldt returned to Chicago and adopted his mother's surname in order to avoid confusion with the English Impressionist, Julius Olsson. After periods of activity in Chicago, Framingham, Massachusetts, and New York, he returned to Europe in 1908, where he was exposed to the work of Henri Matisse and the Fauves. He subsequently abandoned his earlier Whistlerian style in favor of the bright colors, lively patterning, and simplified forms of Post-Impressionism. By the mid-1910s he was incorporating the structural and planar concerns of Paul Cézanne into his work. From 1914 to 1918 Nordfeldt

spent summers in Provincetown, Massachusetts, where he refined the technique of the single block color woodcut and set an example for younger printmakers such as Blanche Lazzell. He moved to Santa Fe, New Mexico in 1919, painting still lifes, portraits of Spanish-Americans, and views of regional scenery (many of which he destroyed). He remained there until 1937, when he relocated to Lambertville, New Jersey. Throughout his career, the artist exhibited widely and taught at a number of art schools. He died in Henderson, Texas in 1955, en route from a trip to Mexico.

George F. Of (1876–1954)

A pioneering figure in the history of American Modernism, George F. Of explored Impressionism, Cubism, and other styles, but he was best known for his fauvist-inspired landscapes. Following the example of Henri Matisse, he used color to communicate a subjective response—in his words, to "create a thing of joy." His paintings were championed by such influential critics as Walter Pach, Willard Huntington-Wright, and Charles Caffin. Born in New York, Of began his career as a framer in his family's business. He initiated his formal training at the Art Students League (1893–98; 1901–02) and then went to Munich, attending classes at the Weinhold School. During a subsequent trip to Paris, he studied at the Delecluse Academy and familiarized himself with contemporary French art. Of returned to New York about 1908 and thereafter divided his time between painting and running his framing business. He fraternized with many artists of the Stieglitz circle, such as Max Weber, Georgia O'Keeffe, and John Marin, and he participated in a number of important modernist shows, notably the *Forum Exhibition of Modern American Painting*, held in 1916.

MacGregor Ormiston (20th Century)

Robert Emmett Owen (1878–1957)

The Impressionist painter Robert Emmett Owen captured the varied moods of rural New England with a vernacular truthfulness that has been likened to the poetry of Robert Frost. Painting old homes and churches, country roads curving through hills and farmland, covered bridges, peaceful waterways, and wooded glades, he created images that epitomized the widespread appreciation in the early twentieth century of New England as the wellspring of American culture and of the nation's identity. Owen was born in North Adams, Massachusetts. He studied there at the Drury Academy, in Boston at the Eric Pape School, and in New York at the Art Students League, the Chase School, and the National Academy of Design. On settling in New York in 1901, Owen became a leading illustrator for prominent magazines, including *Harper's New Monthly* and *Scribner's*. He began to create works that reflected the influence of the American Impressionists Willard Leroy Metcalf, J. Alden Weir, and Childe Hassam. From 1910 until 1920, he lived in Bangall, Connecticut, now part of Stamford, and painted in the open air. After moving back to New York in 1920, Owen opened a gallery on Madison Avenue where he exhibited and sold his own work exclusively. The gallery remained open until 1941, when Owen moved to New Rochelle, New York, and became the artist in residence at the Thomas Paine Memorial Museum. Until the end of his life he continued to paint and to sell his works directly to a large and devoted group of collectors.

Walter Launt Palmer (1854–1932)

The most important artist working in Albany, New York, during the late nineteenth and early twentieth centuries, Walter Launt Palmer painted interiors, still lifes, and views of Venice. However, he was best known for his activity as a landscapist. His snow scenes were especially popular, his sensitive handling of sunlight falling on snow earning him a reputation as the "painter of the American winter." Born and raised in Albany, Palmer was the son of the sculptor Erastus Dow Palmer, who encouraged his early interest in art. In the summer of 1870 he received instruction from the Hudson River School painter Frederic E. Church. Three years later he traveled with his family, visiting the studios of American expatriate painters in France and Italy. He also continued his formal training, studying under the figure painter Charles-Emile-Auguste Durand (Carolus-Duran) in Paris in 1874 and again during 1876–77. Returning to Albany, he began painting detailed and richly colored interiors that were admired in New York art circles for their truthful portrayal of middle-and-upper class American life. After 1887 Palmer turned to landscape themes painted in a tonal Impressionist style. The artist visited Mexico in 1895, Canada and Alaska in 1897, and China and Japan in 1899. He exhibited in the major national annuals throughout the United States, winning numerous awards and prizes for both his oils and watercolors.

Margaret Jordan Patterson

(1867–1950)

A painter, watercolorist, illustrator, and woodblock printer, Margaret Jordan Patterson was born in Soerabaja, Java, the daughter of a Maine sea captain who inspired in her the love of travel she retained for the rest of her life. She grew up in the Boston area and trained at the Pratt Institute in Brooklyn, under Arthur Wesley Dow. She also studied with the Spanish painter Claudio Castellucho in Paris and with Charles Woodbury in Boston, where she was based throughout her mature career. Patterson taught and was an active member of the local art scene. She, nonetheless, found the time to travel abroad often, painting in Holland, Normandy, Spain, Italy, Belgium, and France. She also explored favorite haunts on Cape Cod, Massachusetts, and Monhegan Island, Maine. Her style consisted of a delicate and precise brush handling that she used to portray a range of landscape subjects, including coastal, harbor, and garden scenes. From 1929 until her death, she focused on the vibrant and coloristic properties of flowers in woodblock prints and watercolors. She was also acclaimed for her works in other graphic mediums.

William McGregor Paxton (1869–1941)

A leading member of the Boston School of figure painters, William McGregor Paxton was born in Baltimore, Maryland. In 1889, after attending Dennis Miller Bunker's classes at the Cowles Art School in Boston, he took further instruction at the Académie Julian and the Ecole des Beaux-Arts in Paris, where his teachers included Jean-Léon Gérôme, who influenced his love of detail and sound draftsmanship. Returning to Boston in 1893, he studied with Joseph DeCamp at the Cowles Art School and supported himself by painting portraits. In 1899, after a second trip to Europe, he married Elizabeth Vaughan Okie, a painter of figure subjects and still lifes. Paxton joined the faculty of the Boston Museum School as a drawing instructor in 1906, by which time he had adopted his signature theme—depictions of comely women, ranging from genteel upper-class types to housemaids, which he portrayed in softly lit interiors inspired by the example of the seventeenth-century Dutch painter, Jan Vermeer. Paxton was not only a major figure in Boston; he exhibited regularly in the national annuals in New York, Philadelphia, and elsewhere, and by the mid-1930s had surpassed his contemporaries in the number of popular prizes won. His superbly crafted paintings remained popular with art aficionados in Boston long after modernism had infiltrated the art scene.

Peter Plamondon (b. 1939)

A contemporary painter of still lifes, Peter Plamondon paints objects in common use, such as patterned ceramic dishware, clay pots, and polished stones. Often enlarging these motifs, he derives a purely aesthetic inspiration from them, which he brings out through his abstractly conceived arrangements and his heightening of their coloristic qualities through effects of light and tonal backgrounds. He studied at the San Francisco Art Institute and received his M. F. A. from the School of Fine Arts at Boston University. His work is included in the collections of the Museum of Fine Arts, Boston; the DeCordova Museum; the Worcester Art Museum; the University of California; Chase Manhattan Bank; AT&T; the Boston Public Library; Citibank; Fidelity Mgt. & Research; and Beverly Sills & Peter Greenough.

Joseph Raphael (1869–1950)

Although Joseph Raphael spent most of his life in Europe, he is considered one of the most accomplished and innovative artists to emerge from California. He created a vibrant body of work that evolved over the course of his career, from the naturalist vein of his early work to his masterful images in the modes of Post-Impressionism and Expressionism. After receiving his initial training for six years at the Mark Hopkins Institute in his native San Francisco, he traveled in 1903 to Paris, where he attended classes at the Ecole des Beaux-Arts and at the Académie Julian. Until 1911 he spent half the year in Paris and the other half in Laren, Holland, where an artists' colony had been established. After marrying in 1912, Raphael moved to Uccle, a suburb of Brussels, where he painted his bountiful flower and vegetable garden with a light palette and broad divisionist strokes, reflecting his study in Paris. This vibrant style earned the artist a silver medal at the 1915 Panama Pacific International Exposition, where six of his canvases were displayed. Throughout the 1920s and early 1930s, Raphael sent his works to exhibitions in California, establishing his reputation in the Bay area. In 1934 Raphael moved with his family to Oegstgeest, a suburb of Leiden, Holland. Five years later, when he visited the United States, the outbreak of World War II interfered with his return to Holland. Compelled to remain in his native city, he painted a series of vivid images of the Japanese tea garden in Golden Gate Park along with other local subjects, including a number of scenes of Yosemite that he created at the end of his life. In addition to oils, Raphael produced etchings, woodcuts, and pen and ink drawings.

Lionel S. Reiss (1894–1988)

Born in Austrian-occupied Poland, Lionel S. Reiss moved with his family to New York City in 1898 or 1899. Although he received some instruction at the Art Students League of New York, he was primarily self-taught. During the 1920s he worked as a commercial artist, attracting clients such as Paramount Studios and MGM, for whom he designed the renowned MGM lion. In 1930 he decided to become a fine artist. He subsequently traveled to Europe, North Africa, and the Near East, gathering material for his depictions of Jewish life. His work also includes landscapes, seascapes, and still lifes. He exhibited his oils, watercolors and etchings at the national annuals in New York, Chicago, Philadelphia, and elsewhere and had solo exhibitions at the Midtown Gallery (1939) and the Association of American Artists Gallery (1946). He was the author of *My Models Were Jews* (1938), *New Lights and Old Shadows* (1954), and the illustrator of books such as *A Golden Treasury of Jewish Literature.*

Theodore Robinson (1852–1896)

Theodore Robinson was a leading American Impressionist and an influential member of the Anglo-American art community in Giverny, France. His mature style successfully reconciled modern tenets of light and color with academic precepts of form and structure. Raised in Wisconsin, Robinson studied at the Chicago School of Design (1869–70), the National Academy of Design (1874–76), and in Paris at the Ecole des Beaux-Arts and under Charles-Emile-Auguste Durand (Carolus-Duran). He lived in New York and Evansville, Wisconsin, before returning to France, where he visited Barbizon, Grèz-sur-Loing, and Giverny (1885). In 1887 he helped found the Giverny art colony, becoming friendly with Claude Monet and adopting an Impressionist aesthetic. He settled permanently in New York in 1892 and thereafter painted in upstate New York, New Jersey, Connecticut, and Vermont.

Hugo Robus (1885–1964)

Born in Cleveland, Ohio, Hugo Robus was the son of an iron molder. He inaugurated his formal training at the Cleveland School of Art (1904–08), during which time he worked as a craftsman, manufacturing jewelry, tableware, and ivories. He later studied painting at the National Academy of Design in New York (1910–11) and at the Académie de la Grande Chaumiere in Paris (1912–14), where he also took a course in sculpture with Antoine Bourdelle. Returning to New York in 1914, he taught at the Modern Art School until 1918, when he became a full-time painter, producing expressive, Cubist-inspired figure subjects and interiors. By 1920 he was working as a sculptor, creating abstract figural works characterized by simplified, rhythmic forms, and smooth surfaces. He remained little known in the art world until one of his works was featured in the Whitney Museum of American Art's biennial exhibition in 1933. Thereafter, he exhibited regularly in group shows in New York, Philadelphia, Cleveland, and elsewhere. He also had a number of solo exhibitions, including retrospectives at the Whitney Museum of American Art (1960) and the Forum Gallery in New York (1963–1966). Robus held teaching posts at Columbia University, Hunter College, and the Brooklyn Museum Art School.

Charles Cary Rumsey (1879–1922)

Charles Cary Rumsey was a distinguished American sculptor best known for bronze statues of equestrian and figural subjects created in a style that reflected the French Beaux-Arts tradition. Born into a socially prominent Buffalo, New York, family that had made its fortune in tanning and railroads, Rumsey was at ease throughout his career in fashionable and aristocratic circles. Many of his patrons came from the social elite and his primary subject, polo ponies and their riders, reflected his interest in this sport of the wealthy in which he himself often participated. Rumsey's first studies took place in Paris, where he trained from 1893 through 1895 with the American sculptor Paul Wayland Bartlett. While attending Harvard University, from which he graduated in 1902, Rumsey studied during his summers at the Boston Museum of Fine Arts with Bela Pratt. In Paris he continued his training at the Académies Julian and Colarossi and was advised by Emmanuel Fremiét, a specialist in equestrian statuary and professor at the Jardin des Plantes, who taught him to work from live models and work in plaster, wax, and clay. Returning to America in 1906, Rumsey settled in New York and became established as a creator of animals in bronze, which he produced for a select group of wealthy of Americans, including the railroad magnate, Edward H. Harriman, whose daughter became his wife. Rumsey served as a captain in the U.S. Army in France during World War I. On his return, he became influenced by modernist art, creating his works demonstrating a new monumental and abstract style reflecting the influence of the art of the French sculptor, Aristide Maillol. A skilled polo player, Rumsey played for the U.S. polo team from 1913 until his life was ended suddenly in a car accident in 1922.

Louis Schanker (1903–1981)

Louis Schanker was a painter, printmaker, sculptor, and member of a "protest" group of artists in the 1930s who sought to make American art more experimental and international. Over a career that spanned fifty years, he created purely nonobjective images as well as abstract works that in which he incorporated still life, landscape, and urban elements, often alluding in his images to sports, music, the circus, and socially conscious themes. In 1938 Schanker joined Mark Rothko, Adolph Gottlieb, and other artists in a group opposed to the prevailing styles of regionalism and realism, which became known as "The 10." Schanker was born in New York City. As a youth, he joined the circus and then worked as a laborer in the wheatfields of Canada and the Dakotas. He went on to be a "gandy dancer" on the Erie Railroad and as a stevedore on Great Lakes steamers. For almost a year he rode freight trains with hobos across the country. Schanker ended this peripatetic lifestyle in 1919, when he began attending night classes at Cooper Union, which he continued through 1923. Later he studied in New York at the Art Students League and the Educational Alliance and in Paris at the Académie de la Grande Chaumiere in 1931–32. He spent time in Mallorca in 1933, where he began to incorporate Cubist devices of tilting his planes upward and using prismatic color in his art. After returning home in the mid-1930s, he became a member of the New York City Federal Art Project of the Works Progress Administration. Along with Stuart Davis, he produced a mural for WNYC, the municipal radio station. He also created murals for the Hall of Medicine and the Public Health Building at the New York World's Fair of 1939. Schanker taught printmaking, from 1943 through 1960 at New York's New School for Social Research, and from 1949 through 1964, at Bard College, Annandale-on-Hudson, New York. He also taught at the University of Colorado (1953) and the University of Minnesota (1959).

Charles Green Shaw (1892–1974)

Charles Green Shaw was active as a novelist, poet, and journalist, as well as a painter, associating with such luminaries of the jazz era as F. Scott Fitzgerald, Cole Porter, and Henry Louis Mencken. He was born in New York and studied architecture at Yale University. He received art instruction from the Ashcan painter George Luks and from the Regionalist artist Thomas Hart Benton. While in Europe during the years 1928–32, Shaw formulated a style that combined Cubist design elements with Fauve color and that reflected the aesthetic principles of De Stijl and Neo-Plasticism. On his return to New York in 1932 Shaw developed what he called a "concretionist" style, which involved working with biomorphic shapes of tooled wood, and he created an important series of Cubist-inspired paintings under the collective title, *Plastic Polygon.* In 1937, along with George L. K. Morris and others, Shaw helped found the American Abstract Artists group and served as an important promoter of avant-garde art. Later in his career, his work became more painterly, consisting of monochromatic planes of intersecting color.

Glenn C. Sheffer (1881–1948)

Glenn C. Sheffer was a Chicago-based artist active in the early twentieth century who rendered landscapes, figural works, and decorative compositions in an Impressionist-inspired style. He was also was a noted illustrator. Sheffer was born in Angola, Indiana, and studied at Dennison University (Granville, Ohio), the Art Institute of Chicago, and the American Academy of Art, Chicago. A member of the Chicago Palette & Chisel Club, the Chicago Salon, and the Detroit Scarab Club, Sheffer exhibited at the Detroit Institute, the Art Institute of Chicago, and the Chicago Gallery Association.

Etsuo Shimizu (Japanese, b. 1953)

The Japanese artist Etsuo Shimizu is best known for his oil paintings that vividly reflect the skillfulness of Dutch still-life painting. He earned his undergraduate and graduate degrees in painting at Tama Fine Art University in Tokyo. Since graduating in 1981, he has participated in many solo and group exhibitions in Tokyo. In 1992 Shimizu won first prize in oil painting in a Tokyo Central Museum show.

Eric Sloane (1905–1985)

Eric Sloane was one of America's most multi-talented and prolific artists of the twentieth century. In addition to his many paintings of covered bridges, barns, and abandoned farms, he wrote more than forty books as well as a syndicated column. Originally from New York City, he first worked as a sign painter before studying art at Yale University and the Art Students League. During his travels around the country he became fascinated by covered bridges and old barns, hundreds of which he painted with brilliant clarity. He later wrote and illustrated *American Barns and Covered Bridges* (1954), calling these abandoned barns and ruins, "symbols of American Spirit." Sloane also collected early Americana, from diaries to farm tools, and he featured these objects, especially tools, in other works. During the 1930s his interest in meteorology led to formal study at the Massachusetts Institute of Technology. In 1941 he wrote and published *Clouds, Air, and Wind*, followed later by more than a dozen other books on clouds and weather. Sloane typically worked in a naturalistic style of almost photographic exactitude, alternating with a broader, more painterly treatment in his cloudscapes. Although he preferred exhibiting his work in small gallery settings instead of large group shows, Sloane was elected an academician of the National Academy of Design in 1968, the only year he ever participated in an academy exhibition.

Carlton M. Soule (20th Century)

Albert Sterner (1863–1946)

Albert Sterner achieved international renown as an illustrator, lithographer, and painter. Born in London to an American father and an English mother, he demonstrated an aptitude for drawing as a boy, later winning a scholarship to study at the Birmingham Art Institute. He lived in Germany during 1878–79 and then settled in Chicago, where he worked in various jobs in the field of illustration. In 1886 he went to Paris, refining his skills in depicting the figure at the Académie Julian and the Ecole des Beaux-Arts. In the ensuing years, he became a first-rate illustrator in New York, contributing his drawings to *Century*, *Scribner's*, *Harper's* and other leading periodicals, and illustrating a number of books. In 1895–98 Sterner made an extended trip to Europe, where he was active in Germany, France, and elsewhere. He settled in Nutley, New Jersey, in 1898, devoting his time to portrait drawings and book illustration. He also worked in oil and watercolor and produced a number of monotypes. Sterner moved to Newport, Rhode Island, in 1907, remaining there until about 1915, when he settled permanently in New York City. Praised for his sensitive and versatile draftsmanship, he enjoyed a tremendously successful career, exhibiting his graphic work and paintings in major exhibitions throughout the United States, Canada, and Europe.

Will Henry Stevens (1881–1949)

Born in Vevay, Indiana, Will Henry Stevens studied at the Cincinnati Art Academy and at the Art Students League of New York. In 1921 he joined the faculty of Newcomb College in New Orleans, where he taught until 1948. He also operated his own summer art school in Gatlinburg, Tennessee. During the 1920s, Stevens painted colorful landscapes inspired by Impressionism, but by the following decade he was incorporating elements of Modernism into his work, favoring an expressive use of line, color, and form that he applied to depictions of the American Scene. He eventually adopted a fully non-objective mode of painting that contributed to his reputation as an important Southern abstractionist. The artist died of leukemia in Madison, Indiana, in 1949. A major exhibition of his work was held at the Greenville County Museum of Art in South Carolina in 1987.

Annie Gooding Sykes (1855–1931)

One of several prominent women associated with the artistic life of turn-of-the-century Cincinnati, Annie G. Sykes was lauded for her colorful, Impressionist-inspired watercolors. Born Annie Sullings Gooding in Brookline, Massachusetts, she studied at the Lowell Institute in Boston and at the School of the Museum of Fine Arts during the late 1870s. After her marriage to Gerritt Sykes in 1882, she moved to the "Queen City," continuing her training at the Cincinnati Art Academy from 1884 to 1894. Despite the birth of two children, she continued to balance the demands of home life with her professional aspirations, exhibiting her watercolors locally and in Boston, Chicago, New York, and Philadelphia. On the occasion of her first one-person show, held at the Traxel & Maas Gallery in Cincinnati in 1895, critics praised her fresh, vibrant colors and spontaneous technique, and a reviewer for the *Cincinnati Enquirer* identified her as representing "the new school of impressionism." Sykes's standing among her peers was such that she was often invited to serve on juries of selection with such eminent painters as Frank Duveneck, Maurice Prendergast, and Edward Redfield. She painted in and around Cincinnati, Nonquitt, Massachusetts (where her family had a summer home), Bermuda, Québec, Virginia, and Europe. Her oeuvre includes landscapes and street scenes, but she was most fond of depicting the floral environment.

Allen Tucker (1866–1939)

Allen Tucker was born in Brooklyn and received training as an architect, a profession he practiced until 1904 when he became committed to painting. He was initially inspired by John Henry Twachtman, with whom he studied at the Art Students League. The work of Claude Monet and Vincent van Gogh also strongly influenced him. He worked primarily in New York, but traveled extensively in Europe, especially France. In 1911 he became a charter member of the Association of American Painters and Sculptors, the organization that was responsible for presenting the influential 1913 Armory Show. He participated in the exhibition as well as headed the committee that produced the catalogue; he was also involved with the Society of Independent Artists, the Whitney Studio Club, and served as an advisor to Juliana Force, director of the Whitney Museum. An instructor at the Art Students League from 1921–1926, he also produced a significant body of critical writing including a book, *Design and the Idea*. His first one-person show was held in 1918 at the Whitney Studio Club, and that institution also presented his memorial exhibition in 1939.

P. Valeri (19th Century)

Stuyvesant Van Veen (1910–1988)

Stuyvesant Van Veen was a prominent New York oil and mural painter who created allegorical and realist images of New York and other urban environments. He is celebrated for his series of paintings that commemorate the Brooklyn Dodgers (1963; Ebbets Field Apartment Complex, Brooklyn) and for his masterful rendering of Pittsburgh in *Pittsburgh Panorama*, a mural commissioned by the United States Treasury in 1937 for the adjoining courthouse and post office in Pittsburgh. Van Veen was born in New York City and studied at Pennsylvania Academy of the Fine Arts, the National Academy of Design, the Art Students League (where he worked with Thomas Hart Benton), the New York School of Industrial Art, and Columbia University. He lived in Cincinnati during the mid-1940s, but moved back to New York by 1949, when he began a long, fruitful career as a painting and drawing instructor at City College of New York. In 1972 he was elected to the prestigious American Academy and Institute of Arts and Letters. He exhibited widely during his lifetime and was a member of many professional organizations, including the National Society of Mural Painters, the Artists Equity Association, of which he was president in 1958–59; the American Watercolor Society, the National Institute of Arts and Letters; and the American Artists' Congress.

Jan Voerman, Jr. (Dutch, 1890–1976)

Jan Voerman, Jr. was born in Hattem, Holland, the oldest son of the landscape painter Jan Voerman, Sr. and Anna Verkade (daughter of Enricus Verkade of the chocolate factory), and he grew up in a home that was a social center for artists, poets, and actors. Taught to paint by his father, the younger Voerman was stimulated by his native region's plant life, developing a life-long interest in flora and fauna. By the age of fifteen he was already a professional painter, and completed a commission for illustrations of the Verkade factory, depicting the village of Hattem and its environs. From 1907 to 1940 he painted flowers and landscapes for the Verkade-albums, annual cards produced by a select group of Dutch artists that were sold together with Verkade products such as biscuits and chocolates. The Verkade cards and albums remain collectors' items today. In 1913 Voerman moved to Amster-

dam and studied at the Royal Academy of Fine Arts. His training was cut short by the outbreak of World War I, and Voerman returned to Hattem a year later to continue his study at home. In 1925 he moved to Overveen, where he concentrated on painting plants, birds, and butterflies. He settled in Blaricum in 1933, where he remained until his death. While Voerman's father was famous for his landscapes of Dutch meadows, Jan Jr. excelled at painting the little things in nature: insects, mushrooms, flowers, and birds. He was very successful in his lifetime and exhibited widely in Holland. Probably the greatest honor he received was in 1974 when the Voerman Museum in Hattem opened featuring the work of father and son.

John C. Vondrous (1884–1935)

Born in Prague, then Czechoslovakia, John C. Vondrous was a painter, illustrator, and etcher, known to have rendered city views and harbor scenes. After immigrating to New York at some point in the early twentieth century, he studied at the National Academy of Design under Edward M. Ward, George Maynard, Francis Coates Jones, and John D. Smillie. He spent summers painting on the New England coast, working in Gloucester and Provincetown, Massachusetts. Vondrous received medals at both the Panama-Pacific Exposition (1915) and the Sesqui-Centennial Exposition, Philadelphia (1926). He exhibited at the Art Institute of Chicago and the National Academy of Design.

Frederick Judd Waugh (1861–1940)

Frederick Judd Waugh was one of the most popular and accomplished marine artists of his time. Born in Bordentown, New Jersey, he derived inspiration from his parents who were both artists before enrolling at the Pennsylvania Academy of the Fine Arts. There from 1880 to 1883, he was a pupil of Thomas Eakins and Thomas Anshutz. He continued his training in Paris at the Académie Julian, before returning to Philadelphia in 1885, where he began to paint portraits and landscapes while also creating commercial work for the firm of Dakin and Petrie. After his marriage in 1892, he left for Europe, where he developed his love of the sea while visiting the Island of Sark in the British Channel Islands. He spent the subsequent ten years in London, where he mainly painted figural compositions, which he exhibited at the Royal Academy. However, he continued to create marine scenes, particularly at St. Ives in Cornwall. Returning to America in 1905, Waugh set up a studio in New York. In 1909 he was elected an associate member of the National Academy of Design, and in 1911 he was made an academician. Because of his knowledge of the sea and ships, during the first World War, he was called into the service of the navy for camouflage work. In addition to oils, Waugh created watercolors and wrote a children's book in 1916 entitled *The Clan of Munes*. From 1920 onward, he sent summers in Kent, Connecticut.

Elisha Kent Kane Wetherill (1874–1929)

A painter and etcher, Elisha Kent Kane Wetherill was born in Philadelphia. After studying at the Pennsylvania Academy of the Fine Arts he went to Paris, where he attended classes at the Académie Julian and at James McNeill Whistler's Académie Carmen. Wetherill eventually settled in New York City. His seascapes, urban scenes, and figure subjects were exhibited there, as well as in Philadelphia, Washington, D.C., and elsewhere. A member of the National Academy of Design (A.N.A. 1927), the Salmagundi Club, and Allied Artists of America, the artist died in Aberdeen, South Carolina of injuries suffered during the First World War.

John Whalley (b. 1954)

A contemporary painter of realist imagery, John Whalley is known for responding to what he refers to as "the beauty that speaks softly" in each of his subjects. In his images of fruit, leaves, as well as figures and landscapes, he reveals the goodness and beauty imbued within his motifs. Born in Brooklyn, Whalley studied at the Rhode Island School of Design, majoring in illustration and minoring in drawing and painting. He began to paint fulltime in 1976, settling first in Bridgewater, Massachusetts. After the birth of their two sons, the Whalley family moved to Standish, Maine, where Whalley completed a series of oil paintings and began working in a large format on his graphite still lifes. While in Maine, he became involved with Renaissance International, an assistance organization in Fort Lauderdale, Florida, which prompted him to move there for research on the needs of homeless children in El Salvador. Since 1987 the Whalleys have blended their work in the fine arts with teaching and a commitment to providing a home and a future for the "street children" of the United States and Central and South America.

Andrew Winter (1892–1958)

A painter of forceful depictions of maritime New England, Maine in particular, Andrew Winter was born in Sindi, Estonia, in 1892. He abandoned a planned art career when war broke out, and from 1914 to 1916, he served in a number of British vessels. He then sailed on various American ships until 1921, when he decided to settle in the United States and resume his art education. In that same year, he enrolled in classes at the National Academy of Design in New York. During the Depression, Winter painted many oils on commission for the U.S. Treasury Department. He also executed a large mural portraying maple sugaring for the Wolfeboro, New Hampshire, post office. It was during this time that Winter made his first trip to Monhegan, a small island off the coast of Maine, where he joined a thriving colony of artists who summered at the "Trailing Yew" guesthouse. After spending a number of seasons painting on the island, Winter decided to move there permanently in 1940. He promptly built a studio on a bluff overlooking the Atlantic. He also went on frequent sailing trips with local fishermen. His renderings of local land and seascape, characterized by an emphasis on bold, rugged shorelines, a powerful "Monhegan" light and a tendency to depict man in his battle against the elements of nature, have often been compared to the work of Winslow Homer.

Theodore Wores (1859–1939)

Renowned for his pictorial investigations into exotic and foreign cultures, Theodore Wores was the most important painter working in San Francisco at the turn of the last century. A native of that city, he attended the California School of Design before going to Munich in 1875, where he resumed his training at the Royal Academy and fraternized with artists such as Frank Duveneck and William Merritt Chase. In 1879 he became one of the "Duveneck Boys" who painted together in Florence and Venice and met the painter James Abbott McNeill Whistler, who introduced him to the art of Japan. Following his return to San Francisco in 1881, Wores depicted the Chinatown district and taught at the local Art Students League. He also traveled widely, including taking extended trips to Japan, where he painted portraits and landscapes in a style noted for its vivid chromaticism and impressionistic light effects. His articles on Japan were published in *Century* and *Scribner's*. Wores was also active in Hawaii and Samoa (1901), Spain (1903), the Canadian Rockies (1913), and the Southwest (1915). About 1918 he turned his attention to regional scenery, producing Impressionist-inspired landscapes and his so-called "Blossom Paintings."

William Zorach (1887–1966)

Am important figure in the history of American modernism, William Zorach was active as a painter, sculptor and teacher. Born in Lithuania, he grew up in Cleveland, Ohio. In 1910, after studying in art schools in Cleveland and New York City, he went to Paris, where he received instruction from the Post-Impressionist painter John Duncan Fergusson. It was at Ferguson's school that he met the painter Marguerite Thompson, who introduced him to Paris's vanguard art scene. Zorach subsequently abandoned his naturalist approach and adopted a style characterized by the use of stylized forms, pure color, and variegated brushwork. Returning to New York in 1912, he married Thompson and aligned himself with the local avant-garde, exhibiting his work at the Armory Show of 1913 and at other shows devoted to the promotion of progressive art. He began experimenting with sculpture in 1917, and by 1921 had taught himself to carve stone directly, rather than making a preliminary study in clay. Employing traditional motifs, such as the theme of the mother and child, he developed a personal style notable for its simple, monumental forms and textural variation. Zorach joined the faculty of the Art Students League in 1929, remaining an influential teacher there for over thirty years. He was the author of *Zorach on Sculpture* (1947) and *Art is My Life* (1967).